Sophocles
Antigone

Sophocles
Antigone

A new translation and
commentary by David Franklin
and John Harrison

Introduction to the Greek Theatre
by P.E. Easterling

Series Editors: John Harrison and Judith Affleck

CAMBRIDGE UNIVERSITY PRESS
Cambridge, New York, Melbourne, Madrid, Cape Town, Singapore,
São Paulo, Delhi

Cambridge University Press
The Edinburgh Building, Cambridge CB2 8RU, UK

www.cambridge.org
Information on this title: www.cambridge.org/9780521010733

First published 2003
7th printing 2008

Printed in the United Kingdom at the University Press, Cambridge

A catalogue record for this publication is available from the British Library

ISBN   978-0-521-01073-3 paperback

ACKNOWLEDGEMENTS
Thanks are due to the following for permission to reproduce photographs:
p. 1 ©British Museum; pp. 6, 24, 32, 74, 94 Rex Features; pp. 10, 62 Donald
Cooper/Photostage.
Every effort has been made to reach copyright holders. The publishers would
be glad to hear from anyone whose right they have unknowingly infringed.

Map on p. ix by Helen Humphreys.
Cover picture: detail from *Antigone* by Marie Spartali Stillman, courtesy
of the Simon Carter Art Gallery, Woodbridge, Suffolk, UK/Bridgeman
Art Library.

PERFORMANCE
For permission to give a public performance of this translation of *Antigone*
please write to Permissions Department, Cambridge University Press,
The Edinburgh Building, Shaftesbury Road, Cambridge CB2 8RU.

Contents

Preface

The aim of the series is to enable students to approach Classical plays with confidence and understanding: to discover the play within the text.

The translations are new. Many recent versions of Greek tragedy have been produced by poets and playwrights who do not work from the original Greek. The translators of this series aim to bring readers, actors and directors as close as possible to the playwrights' actual words and intentions: to create translations which are faithful to the original in content and tone; and which are speakable, with all the immediacy of modern English.

The notes are designed for students of Classical Civilisation and Drama, and indeed anyone who is interested in theatre. They address points which present difficulty to the reader of today: chiefly relating to the Greeks' religious and moral attitudes, their social and political life, and mythology.

Our hope is that students should discover the play for themselves. The conventions of the Classical theatre are discussed, but there is no thought of recommending 'authentic' performances. Different groups will find different ways of responding to each play. The best way of bringing alive an ancient play, as any other, is to explore the text practically, to stimulate thought about ways of staging the plays today. Stage directions in the text are minimal, and the notes are not prescriptive; rather, they contain questions and exercises which explore the dramatic qualities of the text. Bullet points introduce suggestions for discussion and analysis; open bullet points focus on more practical exercises.

If the series encourages students to attempt a staged production, so much the better. But the primary aim is understanding and enjoyment.

This translation of *Antigone* is based on the Greek text edited by Hugh Lloyd-Jones and N.G. Wilson for Oxford University Press.

John Harrison
Judith Affleck

Background to the story of
Antigone

(*The names of characters who appear in this play are printed in* **bold**.)

Antigone, like many Greek tragedies, is set in Thebes. The early history of Thebes was the subject of a cycle of epic poems, which provided material for many plays, of which, in addition to *Antigone*, Aeschylus' *Seven against Thebes*, Sophocles' *Oedipus Tyrannus*, *Oedipus at Colonus* and Euripides' *Phoenissae* survive. The dramatists freely adapted the legends, and the version of the story below comes mainly from *Oedipus Tyrannus*, which was written later than *Antigone*.

The city, according to legend, was founded by Cadmus, who came from Phoenicia. He was told by an oracle to found a city in a place to which he was led by a cow. Where the cow lay down, he killed a dragon and sowed its teeth, which sprang up from the ground as armed soldiers, who became the Theban nobles. After a successful reign Cadmus left for western Greece with his wife Harmonia.

An early king was Labdacus, who died when his son Laius was a child. While still a minor, Laius kidnapped Chrysippus, son of Pelops, king of Elis. Pelops pronounced on him a curse, which was to blight the next two generations of the family, the descendants of Labdacus.

When Laius became king and married Jocasta, he was warned that his son would kill him. So he pierced the baby's ankles, tied the feet together and abandoned him on Mount Cithaeron, the common grazing ground of Thebes and neighbouring Corinth. There a Corinthian shepherd found the baby and took him to his king, Polybus, and Queen Merope, who named him Oedipus (Swollen Foot) and brought him up as their own son. But, when an adult, Oedipus, hearing rumours that he was not the king's legitimate son, went to the oracle at Delphi to find out who his parents were. The oracle simply told him that he would kill his father and marry his mother. Oedipus, deciding that the best way to avoid this destiny was not to return to Corinth, travelled towards Thebes. At a crossroads he became involved in a quarrel with some other travellers and in the ensuing fight killed the occupant of a carriage, not knowing it was his own father Laius. Arriving in Thebes he found the city in turmoil, its king missing and the city plagued by the Sphinx, a winged creature with a woman's face and a lion's body.

Creon, the regent and brother of Jocasta, offered the kingdom and his sister's hand in marriage to the man who could solve the Sphinx's riddle and so save the state. Oedipus solved the riddle, and unwittingly married his own mother, by whom he became father of two sons, Eteocles and Polyneices, and two daughters, **Antigone** and **Ismene**.

Years later, Thebes was afflicted by a plague. In answer to Oedipus' enquiry, the oracle at Delphi declared that the land was polluted by the murderer of Laius; only by his removal could the plague be lifted. Oedipus, cursing the unknown murderer and pronouncing him an exile, set in train an enquiry. At each stage it became clearer that he himself was the source of pollution: that he had killed his own father and married his mother. Oedipus put out his own eyes as punishment, Jocasta hanged herself and Creon again became regent.

Oedipus' two sons, approaching adulthood, quarrelled as to which should be king; finally they agreed that they should rule in alternate years, starting with Eteocles. Polyneices went to Argos, where King Adrastus gave him in marriage his daughter Argeia, and, when it became clear that Eteocles did not intend to relinquish the throne, undertook to restore Polyneices to power in Thebes. Adrastus gathered an army, led by seven champions, who fought at the seven gates of Thebes against seven chosen Theban warriors. Eteocles and Polyneices fought one another at the Hypsistai gate and killed one another. The Argives were routed.

Creon, as the nearest surviving kinsman, now became king and decreed that Eteocles should be buried with all honour, but that the corpse of Polyneices should be left to rot on the plain. At this point in the story the action of the play begins.

Map of Ancient Greece

List of characters

ANTIGONE — *daughter of Oedipus*

ISMENE — *daughter of Oedipus*

CHORUS — *Theban elders*

CREON — *new king of Thebes, uncle of Antigone and Ismene*

SENTRY

HAEMON — *Creon's son*

TEIRESIAS — *a blind old seer*

FIRST MESSENGER

EURYDICE — *Creon's wife*

SECOND MESSENGER

Detail from a vase (c. 380–370 BC) showing a scene from the play.

1

PROLOGUE (1–90)

All Sophocles' extant plays begin with a scene involving two or more characters. The setting here is an open place, at dawn (13). Antigone and Ismene come from the gates of the palace (16). Euripides preferred to begin with a single character explaining the background to the play. Here Sophocles presents a dialogue between two sharply differentiated characters, and we learn the details of the situation gradually.

1 My own dear sister No translation can convey Antigone's unusual way of addressing her sister (literally 'very-sister of common blood'), which stresses the closeness of the tie of kinship.

1–2 the sufferings bequeathed by Oedipus Oedipus' crimes (see Background to the story, page vii) had infected Thebes with pollution (see note on page 14), for which Zeus, the supreme deity (see note on page 10), might exact retribution from subsequent generations. Now there is yet another, new misfortune.

6 the general Creon is now the king (155, 167). He had been regent when Oedipus' sons were young; when they shared the throne, he served in the army and is credited with saving Thebes from the Argive attack (1120). Antigone's impersonal reference to her uncle is significant; and by calling him 'general', she suggests that Thebes in the immediate aftermath of the war is under some sort of martial law: the general governs by decree (6, 22, 26, 28, 158, 182, 190).

- Notice the number of questions in Antigone's opening speech. What does this suggest about her manner and emotional state?

Friends and enemies

9 those we love (*philoi,* also 11) embraces all family and close friends, whom one had an obligation to help and protect, whereas it was considered perfectly acceptable to hate or harm anyone who was one's enemy. This could extend to denying them burial, as Creon has to all the Argives. Antigone objects to her brother, her *philos*, being treated as an enemy. In Sophocles' *Ajax* the Greek generals similarly refuse burial to Ajax, their disgraced colleague.

12 double blow The unique, incestuous way in which Eteocles and Polyneices died is stressed (see also 50–1, 166 and note on 140–2).

13 Argive army See Background to the story (page vii).

15 outside Greek women were expected to spend most of their time in the home. For the two sisters to be out of doors creates an atmosphere of secrecy and suggests that things are not normal (see also note on 1141).

ANTIGONE My own dear sister, Ismene, of all the sufferings
bequeathed by Oedipus, can you think of one that Zeus has
not given the two of us in our lifetime? There is no pain, no
ruin, shame or dishonour that I have not seen in your
sufferings and mine.   5
And now, what is this proclamation they say the general has
just made to the whole city? Do you understand it? Have you
heard it? Or don't you yet know that punishment fit for
enemies is coming to those we love?

ISMENE Not a word has come to me, sweet or painful, Antigone,   10
about our loved ones; not since our two brothers were torn
away from us, dying on the same day by a double blow. Since
the Argive army left, just last night, I know of nothing new;
whether good fortune is coming, or more suffering.

ANTIGONE I was right; that is why I brought you outside the   15
palace gates, to hear the news in private.

ISMENE What is it? You are clearly troubled by your news.

ANTIGONE Is Creon not honouring one of our brothers with
burial, and leaving the other in disgrace? He has buried
Eteocles in the ground, they say, observing justice and custom,   20
so that he is honoured among the dead below.

Honours due to the dead

Antigone is concerned to pay her brother due honour (*timē*, 21). The honour due to a dead man was to have his body washed and dressed (see 868) by women of his family and to be burnt or buried, with appropriate libations (see note on 401) and formal laments sung by women (see also note on 1156). To leave a corpse unmourned and unburied, as carrion for birds and beasts of prey, was to treat it, and so the gods of the underworld (67), with dishonour. But Athenian law in the 5th century BC allowed that burial in Attic soil could be refused to those guilty of sacrilege, treason or tyranny.

25 delicious Antigone's bitterness is reflected in her language; see also the sarcastic description of Creon as 'noble' (26).

27 to you and me The edict applies to all citizens (7) but to the sisters in particular, who, as the last survivors of the family, would be responsible for the funeral rites.

● What do the words **to me, I tell you** reveal about Antigone?

30 public stoning by the citizens is a particularly violent punishment; it may seem to Creon apt for a public enemy.

The demands of nobility

Antigone expresses the view (32) that those of noble birth should show superior moral qualities. The incestuous nature of the sisters' birth – Oedipus was married to his own mother (47) – seems not to affect Antigone's view of her own nobility, which she is concerned to prove. She thinks it requires her to honour her brother – even at the cost of her life (32, 42, 63–4, 87–8). This is an extreme view: though the Greeks in general thought it important to honour the dead with burial, we have no evidence that they would risk their own death to achieve it (see the Chorus' view, 204). They were familiar with the practice of casting out without burial those guilty of certain crimes, including treason, so we cannot assume that they would applaud Antigone's extreme position.

The position of women

A woman was normally always under the authority of a male. Before marriage her male authority (*kurios*) was her father or next of kin; once married, her *kurios* was her husband. Women could not vote, stand for office or speak in the law courts; they probably were not admitted to the theatre. For a young woman to flout the authority of her *kurios* as Antigone does would be extraordinary in the Athens of Sophocles' time. Ismene's more 'normal' attitude, accepting women's conventional 'bounds' (60), throws into relief Antigone's stance.

But they say it has been proclaimed to the citizens that, after
his miserable death, the body of Polyneices must not be buried
in a tomb, nor mourned; he is to be left unlamented, unburied,
a delicious hoard for the watching birds to feast on!   25
This is the proclamation that they say the noble Creon has
made to you and me – to me, I tell you – and he is coming
here to make the announcement clear to those who do not
know. He does not treat the matter lightly; whoever disobeys
him in any respect will face death by public stoning in the city.   30
Now you know how things stand; soon you will show whether
you are noble by birth, or a coward from a noble family.

ISMENE My poor sister, if this is how things are, what can I do to
    prevent or change them?

ANTIGONE Consider whether you will share the work and the   35
    action with me.

ISMENE What work? What are you risking? What do you mean?

ANTIGONE Will you lend your hands to mine, to lift the body?

ISMENE What? You intend to bury him, when it has been
    forbidden to the city?   40

ANTIGONE Yes, my brother and yours, even if you wish he were
    not. I will not be caught betraying him.

ISMENE You dare? When Creon has forbidden it?

ANTIGONE It is not for him to keep me from my own.

ISMENE Ah! Think, sister, how our father died: hated, disgraced,   45
    driven by the crimes he had himself uncovered to tear out both
    his eyes with his own hands. Then mother – his mother and
    wife, a double title – destroyed her life with a twisted noose.
    Then the third disaster: our two brothers in a single day
    wrought their shared destiny at each other's hand, the   50
    wretched pair, shedding their own blood.

Ismene's point of view

Ismene tries to make Antigone see the situation realistically, in the context of the state: she talks of the city (40), and citizens (69), the law (53), the power of the king (54, 56); she describes in graphic detail the family disasters, and talks of the weakness of women (55). Death by stoning would be a fate even worse than all the horrors which the sisters have already suffered (52–3). She acknowledges the claims of the dead (58), but bows to superior force.

Moral issues were the subject of much debate in Sophocles' time. Ismene's views seem to relate to the argument that 'Might is Right', a view vigorously expressed in Book 1 of Plato's *Republic* by Thrasymachus, who claims that 'right' is simply a code of behaviour imposed on a state by its ruler (see also note on 197).

Human and divine law

In the striking oxymoron **the crime of holy reverence** (65) Antigone sets out the debate which underlies the conflict of the play: what human law forbids may be a pious act. By burying Polyneices, Antigone claims to be not only paying the honour due to her brother, but also respecting the laws honoured by the gods (67). See note on page 34.

76 You will be much more hateful Antigone still treats her brother as a *philos*, though he was a traitor; but in hating Ismene, she begins to treat her as an enemy (see note on 9, also 85).

- How different is Antigone's attitude to her sister from Creon's treatment of Polyneices?

Antigone and Ismene, New York Shakespeare Festival production 1982.

And now the two of us left alone – think how we will die, most miserably of all, if in defiance of the law we transgress the decree and power of the king. We must remember that we were born women, not to fight against men; and that since we are ruled by stronger hands, we must listen in this matter, and in others still more painful.

I, at least, will beg those beneath the ground to forgive me, since I am coerced in this; I will obey those who are in power. It is senseless to overstep our bounds.

ANTIGONE I will not press you. Even should you wish to do it in the future, I would not be pleased to have you work with me. Be as you will; but I will bury him. It is noble for me to die doing this. I will lie there with him, loved by the one I love, guilty of the crime of holy reverence. I will have to please those below longer than those here, for there I will lie forever. You, if you like, go on dishonouring the laws honoured by the gods.

ISMENE I do not dishonour them; but I am powerless to act against the citizens.

ANTIGONE You can hold on to that excuse; but I will go to raise a burial mound for the brother I love.

ISMENE No, poor woman! I am so afraid for you!

ANTIGONE Do not fear for me; look after your own fate.

ISMENE At least don't reveal what you do to anyone; keep it secret, and I will do the same.

ANTIGONE No! Shout it out! You will be much more hateful for your silence, if you don't proclaim it to everyone!

87 this terrible fate Antigone is ironic – 'this disaster you speak of'.

Antigone's exit
Antigone's departure alone for the open country would have made a striking exit in the Greek theatre (see note on 15).

Antigone and Ismene
- Examine Antigone's arguments. What makes her determined to bury her brother?
- What are Ismene's arguments for refusing to help Antigone? Do they seem reasonable? Is she just being weak, or saying that Antigone is in the wrong?
- With which of the two characters do your sympathies lie?
- What does Antigone's language tell us of her emotional state?
- What impression do you get of Antigone from this scene? Heroic? Reckless? Fanatical? Noble? Foolhardy? Intemperate?
- How would you describe her treatment of Ismene?
- What are Ismene's feelings towards Antigone?
- What are the dramatic advantages of beginning the play with a dialogue of this sort?

PARODOS (ENTRY OF THE CHORUS) (91–158)
At the time of the first production of *Antigone* there would have been fifteen chorusmen. They would have entered, singing this ode, from the sides (*parodoi*) and spent the rest of the performance in the open space of the *orchēstra* (see Introduction to the Greek Theatre, page 110). Viewed from above by the audience in the tiered seating, their dance and choreographed movement were an important element in the expressiveness of Greek theatre. Lyrical passages (in which the words were sung) are centred in the text.

As the sisters separate – Ismene going into the palace, Antigone leaving to bury her brother – the Chorus of Theban elders enter. Subsequent references to them (799, 904, 962) suggest that they are of noble birth. They have been summoned to hear Creon's proclamation (157). In highly figurative language, with many echoes of epic poetry, they salute the dawn, and exult in their victory over the Argives. (For the details see the Background to the story, page vii.)
- At this moment of private tension, what is the effect of the arrival of these men in a mood of public celebration?

95 Dirce One of the rivers of Thebes.

98 The white-shielded soldier The coming of dawn ('eye of the golden day' 94) allowed the Thebans to contemplate the rout of the Argive troops, who carried white shields.

ISMENE You have a hot heart for chilling deeds.

ANTIGONE But I know that I am pleasing those I should most
   please.   80

ISMENE If you are really capable of it; but you are in love with the
   impossible.

ANTIGONE When I have no strength left, then I will stop.

ISMENE Even to start to pursue the impossible is wrong.

ANTIGONE If you say that, you will earn my hatred, and be hated   85
   by the dead man too – and rightly. Allow me and my folly to
   suffer this terrible fate; for I will suffer nothing as bad as an
   ignoble death.

ISMENE Go, if you will. But be sure that, though you are mad to
   go, you are truly dear to those who love you.   90

CHORUS   Rays of the sun!
               Fairest light that has ever dawned
                    Over seven-gated Thebes,
         You appear at last, eye of the golden day,
               Rising above Dirce's streams!   95
                  You have driven headlong
                    In bridle-tearing flight
         The white-shielded soldier who came from Argos
                    In all his battle array.

102 Polyneices There is a play on the meaning of the name: literally 'man of many quarrels'.

103 eagle The image of the bird (white wings) is blended with that of the Argive army, and then into the picture of an eagle attacking and being repelled by a dragon (118) (for the identification of Thebes with a dragon, see Background to the story, page vii).

114 the god of fire was Hephaestus.

116 Ares, the god of war (who favoured the Trojans in the Trojan War) has also helped the Thebans (132–3).

Zeus

In the battles of Greek myth, the gods took sides and regularly intervened. **Zeus who turns battles** (137) has supported the Thebans. As the supreme deity, reigning on Mount Olympus, and god of justice, he punished arrogant pride (*hubris*) – any attempt by mortals to go beyond their natural and rightful lot. The arrogance of the Argives (119, 122) incurred his displeasure, which Zeus, being originally a sky-god, showed with his thunderbolt (123). Zeus had many other roles: guardian of law and morals, of suppliants, guest-friends, the family and the home, of strangers and beggars, and god of oaths.

124 He struck down the man Though not named, this is clearly Capaneus, one of the seven Argive warriors, whose fall was often represented in art. He boasted that not even Zeus could keep him out of Thebes, and was destroyed by a thunderbolt as he reached the top of the wall.

132 on our right hand In the Greek Ares is called 'our trace-horse'. In the four-horse chariot race the trace (right-hand) horse had to pull hardest at the turning post. So the phrase came to describe a particularly vigorous and valued comrade or ally.

The Chorus, National Theatre production, London, 1984.

He came against our land,   100
Launched by the unresolved quarrel
Of Polyneices; he flew over our land
      Screaming like an eagle,
      Shadowing our country
      With wings as white as snow;   105
      With countless weapons,
And helmets crested with horsehair.

He hovered over our rooftops
      And opened his jaws
      To enclose our seven gates   110
      With his slaughtering spears;
            But he left
Before he could gorge his throat with our blood,
      Before the pine torch of the god of fire
Could take hold of our crown of towers.   115
So fierce was the clamour of Ares raised at his back,
      Too much for him as he fought
      With the dragon of Thebes.

For Zeus hates the boasts of a proud tongue.
      He looked down at them   120
      Coming on in a mighty flood,
      Arrogant in clashing gold;
      And brandishing his lightning,
He struck down the man who was already rushing
To roar his triumph from the highest ramparts.   125

Hurled down, he fell to earth with a crash,
      The man who just now carried a torch
      In the frenzied ecstasy of attack,
      Panting gusting blasts of hate.
      But things went otherwise for him;   130
And against others, too, great Ares rampaged,
      Fighting on our right hand
      To deal them their fate.

136 They set up their trophies Victors in battle commonly hung up armour, taken from the defeated, either at the point of battle or on a temple wall with a dedication to a god, here to Zeus. Our word 'trophy' is derived from the Greek word for 'turn' or 'rout' (*tropē*).

140–2 double-slaying spears The two brothers had quarrelled since childhood. The reciprocal nature of their death, two men of the same flesh and blood, is emphasised in the elaborate phrasing (see note on 12, and 165–6).

144 chariot-thronged Thebes Thebes was famous for its war-chariots, and was credited with their invention.

151 Bacchus (or Dionysus) was born in Thebes, where he was worshipped, often in all-night rites, with ecstatic dancing (150). A choral ode (1075–1114) is dedicated to him. It was at his festival in Athens that the play was originally performed (see Introduction to the Greek Theatre, page 110).

152 here comes the king There are no stage directions in our manuscripts. Entrances are often signalled in this way, partly to identify the characters, partly because of the interval between their being seen and their arrival on stage. The Chorus (unlike Antigone) call Creon 'king' (see 166–7), but stress that he is new to office.

157 council This meeting is out of the ordinary (161–2). Creon's council is like those in Homer's epics, in which a king would consult his council when he felt like it; the councillors had the chance to express opinions, but had no vote or powers.

- What sort of world does the rich language of the Chorus conjure up?
- What is the effect, at this stage, of Sophocles' decision to have a chorus of old men, rather than, say, of female companions of Antigone?
- What has Sophocles achieved by introducing Antigone and Ismene before the elders?
○ What is the overall mood of the ode? What sort of music could be appropriate to accompany it?

Seven commanders at seven gates,
    Like matched against like, 135
They set up their trophies of bronze
    To Zeus who turns battles.
Except for the two filled with hate,
    Born of one father, one mother:
They raised their double-slaying spears 140
    Against each other,
And both took their share of one death.

    But glorious Victory
Has come to chariot-thronged Thebes
    With joy to match our own. 145
    After these wars let us find
    Forgetfulness.
Let us visit all the temples of the gods
    With nightlong dancing and song.
Let him who shakes Thebes with his dancing, 150
    Let Bacchus be our leader!

But here comes the king of the land:
    Creon, son of Menoeceus,
By the new fortunes of the gods
    The new king. 155
What plan is he considering,
To make him summon this council of elders,
    All sent for by one command?

FIRST EPISODE (159–305)

160 the gods Creon dutifully credits the gods with the salvation of the state. The image of the state as a ship is common in Greek thought (see also 179).

Kindred blood-shed

Any killer was polluted by the shedding of blood, and most of all the murderer of a kinsman. The **blood-guilt** (*miasma*, 166) could be cleansed only by ritual purification; it was contagious and could affect a whole community (as in Sophocles' *Oedipus Tyrannus*: Oedipus' unwitting murder of his father caused a plague in Thebes). Creon's treatment of Eteocles (185) suggests that he did not think of him as polluted by his brother's death; perhaps he considered the brothers' killings cancelled one another out.

166–7 I now possess the throne Antigone called Creon 'the general', but his constitutional power is clear. As all the male offspring of Laius' line are now dead, Creon (brother to the dead Jocasta) succeeds to the throne as the nearest surviving male relative.

169 until he is seen Creon's own character is about to be put to this test.

173 someone he loves Creon is clarifying his own values: he can justify his treatment of his kinsman Polyneices by saying he (Creon) puts the state first. But we think of Antigone and the conflict which Creon has provoked.

175–6 I would never stay silent In saying that one must be fearless in speaking out in the interests of the state, Creon is talking about a ruler (169) and about himself (175).

- Does he seem to be upholding in general the right to freedom of speech?

185 every rite … noble dead The rites include libations, liquid offerings poured into the ground, to be drunk by the spirits of the dead (see page 4).

CREON Gentlemen, after tossing the life of our city on the great
waves of the ocean, the gods have safely righted it once more. 160
I sent messengers to summon you here, away from all the
people, because I know that you always respected the power of
Laius' throne, and again, when Oedipus governed the city; and
when he died, you still stood by his children with unwavering
loyalty. Since they died on the same day by a double fate, 165
striking and struck in mutual blood-guilt, I now possess the
throne and all its powers, as I am closest kin to the dead.
It is impossible to learn everything of a man, his soul, his will
and his judgement, until he is seen practising government and
law. A man in command of an entire city, who does not adhere 170
to the best policies, but keeps his mouth closed through fear, is
worthless. I think that now, as I always have done. As for a
man who considers someone he loves to be more important
than his country, I say that he is nothing. May Zeus who
always sees everything be my witness that I would never stay 175
silent if I saw ruin threatening the safety of my citizens; nor
could I make a friend of a man who is hostile to this city.
I know this: that our city is our safety, and it is only when she
sails safely that we can make friendships. By such principles
I will make this city great. 180
So now, in accordance with these principles, I have made a
proclamation to the citizens concerning the sons of Oedipus.
Eteocles, who died fighting for this city, proving himself its
greatest spearsman, will be buried in a tomb and honoured
with every rite that comes to the noble dead. 185

188 to drink blood that he shared Note the 'gothic' language.
● Is it significant that the Chorus have used the same image (113)?

191 lamentation Vengeance is total: not even mourning, normally the duty of relatives, is permitted.

Creon's principles
Creon first reminds the old men of their loyalty to his predecessors. Then in a careful policy statement he lays out the qualities which he admires in a ruler and the principles on which he intends to govern. He has no respect for the man who puts a dear one (*philos*, see note on 9) before the state. Nothing could make him treat as a *philos* someone who is an enemy of his country. The safety of the state (*polis*) is paramount. Those who endanger the state are not real *philoi*.

Antigone claims that the ties of blood are absolute (but see note on 76). Creon was 'closest kin to the dead' (167) and he acknowledges that Polyneices was Eteocles' 'blood-brother' (186); but, he says, in matters that affect the safety of the state, the ties of blood may have to be sacrificed. He proposes as a principle that we should choose our *philoi* on the basis of their conduct in the community (176–7).

Kinship versus the state
Antigone has expressed the traditional bonds of family and kinship, still strong in Sophocles' day. Yet the Greek citizen had other claims on his loyalty – to the state. In an age of frequent wars it was everyone's concern to defend his *polis*, the citizens' guarantee of individual freedom, of the rule of law and civilised life. In democratic Athens the *polis* administered justice, which in earlier times had been settled by feuds based on the natural bonds of the blood tie. The tension between the claims of the state and the family is reflected in a popular debate in Sophocles' time about the relative importance in human affairs of law/custom (*nomos*) and nature (*phusis*). The development of the *polis* created conflicts with traditional values, which the case of Polyneices' burial illustrates. Creon, in limiting the claims of *philia*, is adjusting to this change.
● What do you think of the views which Creon expresses? With which of his views do you think the original (possibly all-male) Greek audience would sympathise?
● Does Creon's way of expressing himself tell us anything about him? Do you detect any unattractive qualities?
● Does our knowing Antigone's intentions affect our attitude to Creon?
○ The danger to Thebes has only just passed (13) and Creon is new to office (155). Attempt both a sympathetic and a hostile performance of his speech.

But his blood-brother, Polyneices, who returned from exile to
the land of his fathers and the gods of his people, prepared to
burn it to the ground, prepared to drink blood that he shared,
and to throw the rest into slavery, this man, it has been
proclaimed to the city, will not be dignified with burial or   190
lamentation. He must be left unburied, a corpse for the birds
and dogs to eat, a disgrace in all eyes. Such is my will; never by
my consent will the worthless stand in higher honour than the
just. But whoever is loyal to this city will be honoured by me in
death as in life.   195

197–8 the power to enact any law The Chorus' way of describing Creon's autocratic power would probably strike an ominous note for the first (Athenian) audience (see note on 463).

200 Lay this burden The Chorus are old, but this excuse may hide a more general reluctance to cooperate (200–6).

203 those who disobey Creon evidently is aware of opposition (see 161, 266–9); he does not suspect Antigone (see 231), but we cannot know this yet.

204 in love with death The Chorus, who are ignorant of Antigone's intentions, ironically remind us of her words (63, 87–8) and recall Ismene's (81).

205 money Tragic tyrants tend to impute gain as a motive for opposition. Creon may be prevented from expanding on this theme (as he does later, 271) by the Sentry's arrival.

The Chorus
- What do we learn of the Chorus from their words to Creon?
- Are they dissociating themselves from Creon's decree or simply being deferential (especially 197–8)?
- Do you sympathise with them?

The Sentry
We have been told (201) that the corpse was guarded, but we are not prepared for the arrival of the sentry (207), who must enter from the same direction in which Antigone went. He is not announced and his circumlocution prevents us being sure what his errand is, until 228. Slaves and characters of humble status are quite common in Greek tragedy: though they – like women – played little part in public life, they had a 'voice' in drama, especially comedy.

210 My spirit was talking to me The inner dialogue is a feature of epic poetry, in which a hero could debate with his spirit (*thumos* or *psychē*), as if it had a sort of independent existence. In *Odyssey ix* Odysseus thinks of killing Cyclops, 'but a second *thumos* checked me'.
- What is the effect of this epic device when used by the guard?

CHORUS Such is your pleasure, son of Menoeceus, in dealing with the enemy and the friend of this city. You have the power to enact any law, both for the dead and for those of us surviving.

CREON So now you must be guardians of my decree.

CHORUS Lay this burden on a younger man. 200

CREON Men are already in position to guard the body.

CHORUS So what is your command, if not that?

CREON That you do not side with those who disobey the decree.

CHORUS No-one is such a fool that he is in love with death.

CREON And indeed that is the penalty. But money often destroys 205 men through their greed.

SENTRY Lord, I will not say that I put enough spring in my stride to arrive out of breath with hurrying. You see, I had many pauses for thought, turning in my tracks to go back where I came from. My spirit was talking to me all the time, saying 210 'Fool, why are you going where you'll be punished for your journey? Wretch, are you wasting time again? If Creon hears this news from someone else, you'll be sure to suffer for it!'

The Chorus salute Creon, production in Poland, 1946.

221 I didn't do it!
- How nervous is the Sentry? (See 213.)

227 Out with it! The Sentry's meandering speech tests Creon's patience.
- What has Creon's reaction been up to now? Amused? Suspicious? Irritated?

229–30 the proper rites See note on 237.

231 man Creon does not imagine it was the work of a woman. The audience naturally assumes that it was Antigone, and can begin to enjoy the dramatic irony of knowing more than a character on stage.

237 a thin layer of dust Antigone had not managed to heap up the mound which she intended (71). She had managed no more than a light covering of earth, suggesting the work of someone seeking to avoid the curse/pollution which one was supposed to incur in passing a corpse without sprinkling earth on it (238). It is not clear whether such a sprinkling was 'symbolic' or did constitute burial.

245 red-hot iron … fire Ancient formulae accompanying oaths.

With these thoughts going round in circles, I got here slowly
with all the delaying; so a short journey becomes long. But in   215
the end, coming to you was the course that won the day. And
even if I have nothing to say, I will say it nonetheless. I come
clutching one hope: that I will suffer nothing other than my
destiny.

CREON What is it that makes you afraid?   220

SENTRY I want to tell you first on my own account: I didn't do it!
    And I didn't see the man who did; so it would not be fair for
    me to come to any harm.

CREON You take careful aim, and barricade yourself against
    blame in the matter. You clearly have something strange to tell.   225

SENTRY Yes, and terrible, which makes me very hesitant.

CREON Out with it! And then be gone!

SENTRY Well, I will tell you. Someone has just buried the body
    and left; he sprinkled dry dust on the flesh, and gave it the
    proper rites.   230

CREON What? What man dared to do this?

SENTRY I don't know. There was no mark of a pickaxe, no earth
    turned over with a spade. The ground was hard and dry,
    unbroken by wheel-tracks; the workman left no trace.
    When the first day-watchman showed it to us, it seemed to us   235
    all like a miracle – but ominous for us. For he had disappeared,
    not in a grave, but just under a thin layer of dust, as though
    someone were trying to avoid a divine curse. There was no sign
    that any wild animal or dog had come near, and the body did
    not look torn.   240
    Then harsh words flew between us, guard blaming guard, and
    it would have ended in blows, with no-one there to stop it.
    Each man in turn was the one who had done it, no-one was
    proven guilty, and everybody pleaded ignorance. We were
    ready to take red-hot iron in our hands, and walk through fire,   245
    and swear by the gods that we had not done it, that we were
    not in league with those who planned or carried out the deed.

Divine intervention?

To the guards the 'burial' is mysterious and inexplicable, 'a miracle' (236). Unaccountably it protected the corpse from animals (238–40). The Chorus, too, tentatively wonder if it may have been the work of the gods (256–7). Creon contemptuously rejects the idea that the gods would care for one who had attacked their temples and their land (258–65), and the idea is not pursued in this scene. But the question has been raised: what is the gods' attitude to the burial? There will be further discussion of this point (see note on 390).

258–9 Stop! … insane as well as senile! The way in which Creon reacts to other characters – and so practises government (169) – helps us to make a judgement about his character.

263–4 temples … their [the gods'] country … laws Religious cults were an integral part of the life of the state. Creon's words, in linking temples and laws, are a natural way of expressing the danger which Polyneices presented to the state of Thebes (see 100–15).

268 under the yoke
● What does this image (see also 'toss their heads', 269) suggest?

Greed and profit

Ancient history is full of examples of conspiracies against tyrants and kings. So it is not surprising that the autocrat in tragedy is often presented as insecure, wary of plots and, especially, afraid of the power of money and the desire for gain. Oedipus in *Oedipus Tyrannus* is prey to these suspicions. Creon, too, appears obsessed by them (205, 271–6, 281–4, 295, 299–300). He is aware (266, see 203) of an opposition to him ('all this time' could refer back to the time when he was regent), and sure that this is motivated by greed and profit (270, 281–4, 295, see 205). His diatribe against money (271–5) is one of the earliest passages in literature to suggest so comprehensively that money is the cause of all evil.

In the end, when any more investigation was useless, one man
spoke, and he made us all bow our heads down in fear. We
could see no way to disagree with him, and no way to come   250
out well if we did as he said. His point was that the deed must
be reported to you, and not covered up. This argument won
the day, and for this privilege the lot chose me – just my luck!
So here I am against my will, and yours, I know that; for no-
one loves the bearer of bad news.   255

CHORUS Lord, all this time my thoughts have been saying that
this might be the work of the gods.

CREON Stop! Before your words fill me with anger, or you will
prove yourself insane as well as senile! What you say is
intolerable, if you mean that the gods care about this corpse.   260
Do you think that they buried him because they honoured him
so highly as a benefactor? The man who came to burn the
pillars and treasures of their temples, to burn their country and
scatter its laws to the wind? Can you see the gods honouring
evil men? Impossible!   265
No, all this time men in the city have been muttering against
me in secret and resenting my rule; instead of keeping their
necks under the yoke and accepting me, as they should, they
toss their heads in rebellion. I understand everything: my
guards have been bribed by these men to carry out this deed.   270
Money! Nothing so evil has ever taken root in mankind. It sacks
whole cities, and wrenches men from their homes; it schools,
corrupts the minds of honest men to commit acts of shame; it
teaches people unrestrained wickedness, to contemplate every
act of evil. But the men who were bribed to carry it out have   275
made sure that in time they will pay the penalty.

277 Zeus still has my reverence There is no reason to doubt that Creon is sincere in his religious belief (see also 160, 174, 263).

280 strung up alive Another sign of Creon's cruelty: criminals, especially slaves, were hung by the arms and flogged, to make them tell the truth.

Creon's character
- How do you react to Creon's confidence (269, 295) that he knows who is responsible for the burial?
- What do we learn about him from his views – and his language (267–9) – on the proper behaviour of citizens?
- What do his threats to the Sentry (277–84) suggest about his character?
- In what sense is Creon a religious man?
○ Look at the language of Creon's speech, especially the long sentence (277–84). Attempt a performance which brings out its climactic tone.

302–5 there's no way ... to the gods! The words are clearly not meant to be heard by Creon, who must have turned to go into the palace.

Creon and the Sentry
The scene offers us a chance to see Creon dealing with a slave, a member of his household.
- What does Creon's manner reveal? How well does he live up to his implied claim (175–6) to respect freedom of speech?
- How well does the Sentry stand up to Creon? What aspects of his language help us to establish his character? What qualities do you detect? Is he terrified, as he implies (249)?
- Are there elements of comedy in the scene?

F. Murray Abraham as Creon, New York Shakespeare Festival production.

As surely as Zeus still has my reverence, know this: I tell you
on oath, that if you do not find the man who carried out this
burial, and produce him before my eyes, death alone will not
be enough for you; first you will be strung up alive, to publicise 280
your crime, so that when you steal in the future you will know
where money should be won, and learn that loving gain from
every source is wrong. You will see that more men are ruined
than helped by corrupt gains.

SENTRY Will you give me leave to speak, or should I just turn and 285
go?

CREON Do you not know, even now, how much your words
offend me?

SENTRY Is it your ears or your soul that they hurt?

CREON Why ask precisely where I feel pain? 290

SENTRY The man who did it offends your soul; I just offend your
ears.

CREON Ah! It is clear that you are a born blatherer.

SENTRY But not the one who did this deed!

CREON You did, and you sold your life for silver! 295

SENTRY No! It is a terrible thing when someone with the power to
judge judges wrongly.

CREON Yes, air your smart opinions! But if you do not produce
the culprits for me, you will agree that corrupt profits bring
pain. 300

SENTRY With all my heart, let him be found! But whether he is
caught or not – and fortune will decide that – there's no way
you will see me back here. Now that I have been saved, beyond
all hope and expectation, I say 'Thanks very much' to the
gods! 305

FIRST CHORAL ODE (1ST *STASIMON*) (306–59)

The Chorus' first song, at their entry, was the *parodos* (91–151). A *stasimon* was a structured ode, sung with dance in the *orchēstra*; often, in tragedy, it brought together in lyric form themes from the preceding section of the play and explored the moral issues involved. This ode, in two pairs of verses, expresses the marvel of man's progress and resourcefulness. The first two verses describe how man has conquered nature and learnt to kill and tame animals.

Conquering nature

From early times there were moralists who warned that sailing (308–10) was a violation of nature, which separated lands by the sea, in order to keep men apart. The Chorus' statement (313) that man, in working the land, 'wears away' an 'inexhaustible' god (Earth) seems also to hint at *hubris* or blasphemy. Yet the strange oxymoron and the positive energy of the language give the verse at least an ambiguous quality.

The second pair of verses (327–50) describes how man developed his intellectual and social skills, to create civilisation; there is only death from which he has found no escape. His skills can be put to good use or bad: if he observes the laws of the state and the justice which men swear by the gods to keep, he makes his state great; the man who recklessly embraces evil has no state.

CHORUS   There are many wonders in the world,
              But none is more wonderful than man.
              He crosses the grey sea,
              Riding the storm winds from the south
              Through the waves that rear around him.   310
              The oldest of the gods,
              Immortal, inexhaustible Earth,
              He wears away,
              Ploughing back and forth, year after year,
              Turning the soil with the horses he breeds.   315

              He snares the lightheaded race of birds,
              And all kinds of savage beasts,
              The sea creatures of the deep
              In the meshing nets that he casts,
              Man the resourceful.   320
              With his skills he masters
              The animals that live in the wild
              And wander the mountains;
              He trains the long-maned stallion
              And the tireless mountain bull   325
              To the yoke upon their neck.

              He has taught himself speech,
              And thought,
              Swift as the wind,
              And the desire to live in a city.   330
              To escape the hard frosts and pelting storms
              Of the open sky,
              He has contrived everything.
              He lacks resources for nothing the future can bring,
              Only from death can he devise no escape,   335
              Though he has discovered cures
              For impossible plagues.

The *polis*

The prosperity of the individual and the state are interlinked. The Chorus' words (342–4) recall those of Creon that 'our city is our safety' (178–9). To be stateless (345) was a dreadful fate: Philoctetes called it 'living death' (Sophocles, *Philoctetes*).

The significance of the ode

Tragedy tends to stress man's subordination to the gods. The tone in which this ode seems to celebrate man's skills, courage, patience and resourcefulness is unusual, reflecting the confident mood of the Athenian democracy and the teaching of the thinkers known as 'Sophists'. The ode is remarkable in suggesting that man's own inventiveness – without reference to divine help – is responsible for human progress: even man's failure to conquer death is seen not as a divine check, but as a matter of fact.

In the context, if the Chorus are reacting to the Sentry's news, they seem to be implying that it is the burier who is 'inventive' (338). It is hard to know with certainty how sincere up to now their support of Creon has been, but a tragic chorus in an ode sometimes explore the wider issues of a play in ways which extend beyond their own dramatic character. The tone of the first three verses does seem positive and admiring; but then, rather than take sides, the Chorus advocate a balance between the claims of the laws of the state and the justice of the gods. (This is another example of the law/nature debate, if the justice of the gods is seen as natural; see page 16.) Whoever indulges in reckless daring (346) can upset the necessary balance: the statement is as relevant to Creon as to the person who has buried Polyneices.

351 god-sent illusion Again (see 256–7) the Chorus think that what they cannot understand may have a supernatural cause.

Antigone's entry

The choral ode covers a lapse of time (see 388). As it ends, the Sentry brings on Antigone (351), possibly with other attendants (see note on 450). The Chorus, still singing, express amazement and sympathy.

○ Would the entry be more effective if the Chorus' sympathetic greeting and questions were ignored by Antigone or not heard by her?

With inventive skill
Beyond all dreams of knowledge,
He makes his way   340
Now to evil, and now again to good.
When he combines the laws of his country
With the justice of the gods he is sworn to,
His city stands tall.
But he has no city at all   345
Who through reckless daring
Lives with evil.
May I not share a hearth
Nor think like thoughts,
With him who does such things.   350

Is this some god-sent illusion?
My mind is torn in two!
How can I deny what I know?
This girl is Antigone!
Oh, wretched child of a wretched father, Oedipus,   355
What is this?
Are they bringing you under arrest,
Disobedient to the law of the king,
And caught in an act of madness?

SECOND EPISODE (360–546)

Creon enters almost immediately (362) from the palace. His and Antigone's inevitable confrontation is delayed by the Sentry.

○ Antigone does not speak until line 411. Is she bound? How would you highlight her silent presence?

○ What is the manner and mood of the Sentry? What is the effect of his talking at length about himself?

371 lots See line 253.

The Sentry's report (383–408)

The Sentry's account of Antigone's arrest contains vivid detail mixed with a simple religiosity (393–4), 'homespun' philosophy (365, 406–7), sensitive imagery (396–7) and a strong sense of character.

● What is the dramatic effect of having this profoundly important news delivered by such a 'simple' character?

385 decaying corpse The guards' orders were to find the culprit. By brushing away the dust they restored the corpse to its unburied state. They may have hoped to provoke the burier to return.

386 a ridge The corpse lies out on a high plain (1153), close to a hill.

390 whirlwind This enabled Antigone to arrive unnoticed. The Sentry's description adds a sense of mystery and again (394, see page 22) hints at divine intervention.

Antigone is discovered covering the corpse of Polyneices in a scene from a Greek film of the play, 1961.

SENTRY This is the one who did the deed; we caught her burying   360
him. But where is Creon?

CHORUS Here he is, coming back out of the palace just when he is
needed.

CREON What is it? What makes my arrival timely?

SENTRY Lord, there is nothing mortals should swear they will never   365
do; hindsight proves us wrong. I swore that I would not return
here in a hurry, after surviving the storm of your threats. But joy
that is prayed for beyond our hope exceeds all other pleasures.
And so I've come, despite the oaths I swore against it, bringing
this girl who was captured performing rites for the dead. This   370
time, no lots were drawn; this is my windfall, and no-one else's.
Now, lord, here she is; take her, question her and pass
judgement. I have the right to go free, and get myself out of this
trouble.

CREON You bring this woman...? Where and in what circumstances   375
did you arrest her?

SENTRY She was burying the man; now you know everything.

CREON Do you understand what you are saying? You are telling the
truth?

SENTRY I saw her burying the body whose burial you had forbidden.   380
Are my words plain and clear?

CREON And how did she come to be seen and caught in the act?

SENTRY This is how it was. When we got there, with your terrible
threats hanging over us, we swept off all the dust that covered the
body, and laid bare the decaying corpse. Then we sat down on   385
a ridge, upwind, so the smell of him wouldn't hit us, shaking
each other to keep awake, with savage threats, if anyone should
be careless about this job. So it went on, until the glaring disc of
the sun stood right overhead and the heat was burning.
Then, all of a sudden, a whirlwind raised a storm of dust from   390
the ground, an affliction from heaven; and it filled the plain,
ravaging all the leaves of the woods, and the whole sky was
choked with it. We closed our eyes, and endured the plague of
the gods.

396 a bird The picture of a grieving girl is reinforced by an emotive image.

● How appropriate is the metaphor?

401 libations Liquid offerings were a traditional way of honouring the dead. In *Odyssey x* Odysseus is told to offer three liquids: honey, wine and water. Here presumably the same liquid is poured three times.

Why did Antigone return to the corpse?

We know neither why Antigone left after the first 'burial', nor why she returned; but she did say that she would continue to honour Polyneices as long as she had strength (83). Possibly (a) she had heard that the corpse had been exposed, the effect of the first sprinkling was nullified and she had to go and cover it again; or (b) the first burial was in some way incomplete (she arrives with a jug and libations); perhaps she wanted to make further offerings, complete the usual lamentation or put on more earth; or (c) in her grief she simply wanted to be at her brother's side.

● Does it matter that we cannot be sure why she returned?

407 people you care for The guard, as a slave of the household, counts Antigone among his *philoi*. 'Good servants share their masters' sufferings' (the Nurse in *Medea*).

409 bending your head
● What is Antigone's mood? Sullen? Modest? Accepting?
○ When does she look up?

411 I admit Antigone never denies her responsibility (404, 415).

Confrontation (*agōn*)

The Greeks delighted in debate, in the law court and in their political assemblies; and this sort of confrontation (*agōn*) became a familiar feature of their drama too. Each protagonist delivers an opening speech, and the debate then usually changes to *stichomythia* (see page 40).

Antigone, handcuffed, being dragged into Creon's palace in a scene from Anouilh's Broadway version of the play.

When after a long time it passed, the girl was seen, and she   395
cried out bitterly, the shrill cry of a bird when it sees its home
empty, its nest stripped of young. So she, when she saw the
body laid bare, raised a mourning cry, and called down terrible
curses on those who had done the deed. At once she brought
dry dust in her hands, and from a fine bronze flask, holding it   400
high, she poured three libations to crown the corpse.
We rushed down when we saw her and quickly cornered our
quarry; but she was not panicked. We questioned her about
her deeds before and now. She stood there and denied nothing,
and for me that was welcome and painful at the same time.   405
It is most sweet to get yourself out of trouble, but painful to
cause trouble to people you care for. But all that matters less to
me than my own safety.

CREON You – you, bending your head to the ground, do you
admit or deny that you have done this?   410

ANTIGONE Yes, I admit doing it; I will not deny it.

CREON You – take yourself off, wherever you like; you are free of
this grave charge. But you, tell me, not at great length, but
briefly: did you know of the proclamation forbidding this?

ANTIGONE I knew. How could I not? It was public knowledge.   415

CREON And yet you dared to break this law?

418 the gods below have the dead in their keeping.

421 unwritten ... laws Among these unwritten laws Antigone puts the duty of burial, ordained by the gods below (see also 67). Such 'laws' probably included the Greek traditions of respect for parents, suppliants and strangers, as well as taboos against incest, oath-breaking and so on. (See also next note.)

Divine and man-made laws
Antigone distinguishes man-made laws, and specifically Creon's proclamation, from the unwritten, universal and eternal 'laws' (421), which she ascribes to the gods. There were gods to oversee the safety and the workings of the state (263), to whom Creon's religious observance – and that of the Chorus in the *parodos* – is directed; and so he dutifully includes Zeus, as god of law and order, in his prayers and oaths (see note on Zeus, page 10). However, Antigone looks to more fundamental obligations, and it is Zeus, as the god who legislates on matters of religion, that she reveres. She would rather defy Creon's edict than offend Zeus and the justice of the gods below, in whose court, if she were to neglect this duty, she would be punished (423). See also note on Kinship versus the state, page 16.

426 if I am to die Antigone is still thinking of a martyr's death (see note on The demands of nobility, page 4), which she describes as a gain, using ironically the word (*kerdos*) which Creon uses for 'profit', the motive which he ascribed to the Sentry (295).

432 a fool This strikingly rude remark echoes that of the Sentry (296–7).
- How aware were you before this speech that Antigone was motivated by this strong religious principle?
- Does this present her in a new light? How would you describe her in this speech?

433 violent See Background to the story (page vii) for Oedipus' story. In *Oedipus Tyrannus* (written after *Antigone*) he reacts in a violent, passionate way when he is challenged by Teiresias.

The Chorus
The Chorus often seem to act as a sort of neutral umpire in conflicts like this, but here they seem clearly critical of Antigone.
- Could the Chorus' words be said in sorrow?
- How does their criticism affect our attitude to Antigone?
- Are the Chorus right (433–4) in their judgement of Antigone, that she is 'violent' and uncompromising?

ANTIGONE Yes; for it was not Zeus who made this proclamation
to me; nor did Justice who dwells with the gods below lay
down these laws for mankind. Nor did I think that your
human proclamation had sufficient power to override the   420
unwritten, unassailable laws of the gods. They live not just
yesterday and today, but forever, and no-one knows when they
first came to light. I was not going to incur punishment from
the gods, not in fear of the will of any man. I knew I must die –
how could I not? – even if you had not made your   425
proclamation. But if I am to die before my time, then I call
that a gain; for someone who lives in the midst of evils as I do,
how could it not be an advantage to die? So for me to meet this
fate is no pain at all. But if I had allowed the dead son of my
mother to remain unburied, then I would have suffered; as it   430
is, I feel no pain. If I now seem to you to have acted foolishly,
perhaps I am convicted of folly by a fool.

CHORUS It is clear; the girl is the violent child of a violent father.
She does not know how to yield in misfortune.

436 iron was tempered (i.e. hardened) by being heated in the fire and then dipped in water.

438 wild-tempered horses Contrast Creon's imagery (see also 268) with the Sentry's (396).

439 slave In no sense was Antigone a 'slave'.
● What does the use of this word tell us about Creon?

Creon's values
In Creon's eyes Antigone is guilty of two acts of outrage (*hubris*, 441–4; see note on Zeus, page 10): by breaking the law and by exulting in triumph (443, 454). His mention of laughter recalls the values of epic and tragic heroes, like Ajax and Achilles, for whom it was all right to laugh at one's enemies. Creon cannot bear being laughed *at*. Medea in Euripides' *Medea* is so obsessed by the thought of her husband's mockery that in revenge for his betrayal of her she kills their children.

Creon, dreading both mockery and the idea of being worsted by a woman (444, see note on 489), will put the two sisters to death. So vehement is he in his determination that no tie of kinship will prevent his punishing them, that his language (445) lacks precise meaning – how can Antigone be any relative but his niece?

447 Zeus was associated with all aspects of the household and family. His altar stood in the centre of the courtyard of the house (see page 10 and note on 618).

448 terrible death Creon is, as far as we know, still bent on the most savage of punishments – death by stoning (30).
● On what evidence does he condemn Ismene?

450 Call her! Presumably there are attendants on stage: they perform similar duties at lines 543 and 710.

453 someone Creon turns to Antigone.

Creon's speech
● How would you describe Creon's response to Antigone's speech?
● What qualities would you say he himself thinks he displays?
● What characteristics do you think he reveals?

CREON Be sure that the most stubborn wills fall hardest; it is the   435
strongest iron, tempered to hardness in the fire, that you will
most often see shattered and broken to pieces. I have known
wild-tempered horses brought to order with a tiny bit. There
is no place for arrogance when you are the slave of those you
live with.   440

She already knew how to commit outrageous deeds when she
broke the laws that had been laid down. The second outrage is
that, having done it, she boasts and laughs at what she has
done. Surely I am not the man now – she is! – if victory goes to
her without punishment. Whether she is my sister's child, or   445
closer to me by blood than any member of my household who
worships Zeus at the altar, she and her sister will not escape the
most terrible death; for I accuse her sister equally of plotting
this burial.

Call her! I saw her inside just now, hysterical, not in control of   450
her wits. The mind tends to convict itself of crimes in advance,
when people scheme wrongdoing under cover of darkness.
And yet I hate it more when someone caught red-handed seeks
to glorify the crime.

ANTIGONE Do you want to do anything more than take me and   455
put me to death?

CREON I do not. When I have done that, I have everything.

459 I pray it never will! Antigone refuses to contemplate that she and Creon are reconcilable.

● Is it their ideas or their personalities which are in conflict?

Antigone as 'heroine'

'Glory' (460) was the aim of Homeric heroes, like Achilles, for whom a short and glorious life was preferable to a long and inglorious one. Antigone seems to see herself in a heroic mould, submitting to what Creon calls a 'foul death' for an honourable and religious cause (63, 423), in defiance of a repressive tyrant (461–4). In periods of political or religious repression her role has been interpreted by some as a champion of freedom or a religious martyr. In the twentieth century the story was used by Anouilh and Brecht in the context of German fascism.

● How valid is such an interpretation?

462–3 if fear did not shut their mouths This is not the first indication that Creon may not have popular support (203, 266–9; see also 467 and 643–50). Antigone may be referring to the group of elders who make up the Chorus or the citizen body.

463 tyranny The word *tyrannis* sometimes simply means autocratic rule, but to the Athenians, who expelled tyrants to establish their democracy, it could imply arbitrary and despotic power. The Chorus have already described Creon's power as absolute (197–8).

465 the descendants of Cadmus are the Thebans. For Cadmus, the legendary founder of Thebes, see Background to the story, page vii.

469 so differently from them Creon seems to mean 'You don't think it necessary to disguise your feelings'. Whereas he seemed in theory to advocate freedom of speech (171, 175), in practice he prefers respectful silence (see also 268).

471 flesh and blood Antigone's language stresses the physical nature of the blood tie (see also 1, 429). But Creon does not avoid using the word 'blood-brother' (472, see also 186), because it does not have the same emotive significance for him.

487 form ties of love

● What exactly do you think Antigone means? Is she claiming in general to love others? Or saying that, even if Eteocles in death still hates Polyneices, she does not join in that hatred? Or is she restating the principle that the bond of kinship is all-important?

ANTIGONE So why delay? There is nothing in your words that
   pleases me – I pray it never will! – and what I say is just as
   displeasing to you. And yet how could I have won greater glory   460
   than by laying my own brother in his grave? I would say that
   all these people here would approve of what I have done, if fear
   did not shut their mouths. But one of the blessings of tyranny
   is its freedom to do and say what it likes.

CREON Of all the descendants of Cadmus, you are the only one to   465
   see it like this.

ANTIGONE These men do too; but they hold their tongues before
   you.

CREON Are you not ashamed to think so differently from them?

ANTIGONE No; there is nothing shameful in honouring my own   470
   flesh and blood.

CREON Was it not a blood-brother that died opposing him?

ANTIGONE Brother by the same mother and father.

CREON So how can you grant an honour that is so disrespectful to
   him?   475

ANTIGONE The dead man will not bear out that view.

CREON He will, if you give him and the traitor equal honour.

ANTIGONE No; it was his brother, not some slave, who died.

CREON Trying to overthrow our country! The other stood in its
   defence!   480

ANTIGONE Nevertheless, Hades desires these rites.

CREON The good man does not want to share the same lot with
   the wicked.

ANTIGONE Who knows whether this is not right in the world
   below?   485

CREON An enemy never earns love, not even in death.

ANTIGONE It is my nature to form ties of love, not of hate.

Creon's misogyny (489)

Creon's concern that women should know their place (544) and his determination not to yield to a woman (444, 489) is to prove obsessive.

- To what extent do you think this aspect of his character determines his behaviour?

Stichomythia

The rhythm of the dialogue in tragedy is regularly varied by passages of one-line exchanges (*stichomythia*). Here it serves to point up the difference between Creon's and Antigone's positions. Creon simply cannot understand her. To him the fact that the patriot and the traitor were of the same blood is irrelevant. He cannot believe that Eteocles would want Polyneices to receive the same treatment (482–3, 486).

- Does Creon try to understand Antigone?
- How strong is Creon's argument (especially 472–7, 486)? How effective is Antigone's answer (484–5, 487)?
- To what extent do you think Creon and Antigone are comparable? In character? In their attitudes?
- How do the two behave in the dialogue?
- Does Creon's remark at 488–9 alter the tone of the exchanges? If so, how do you explain this?

Ismene's entry

The Chorus (490–4) offer a more sympathetic description of Ismene's distress than Creon (450).

495 viper Another animal image from Creon (268, 438). This simile, with its suggestion of treachery and lurid mention of 'drinking blood' (also 188), again convicts Creon of wrong judgement.

500 I did the deed
- How do you explain Ismene's change of attitude? Does she share Antigone's view of death?

519 You chose to live Antigone warned Ismene in the first scene (61–2) that she would not let her be involved in the burial after her first hesitation; by the choice which she made at line 68 (see 502) she betrayed Polyneices. To show love in words alone is not enough (507). Antigone's notion of justice (502) is fixed and immovable.

CREON Then if you must love, go beneath the earth and love them! But a woman will never rule me while I am alive!

CHORUS   Here comes Ismene from the palace,   490
                        Shedding a fond sister's tears.
                              Her face is flushed.
                  The cloud upon her brow mars her beauty,
                        Staining her fair cheeks dark.

CREON You, lurking in my house like a viper, secretly drinking   495
my blood! I didn't know I was rearing two plagues to rise
against my throne. Come on, tell me: will you confess to
having a part in this burial, or will you swear you know
nothing about it?

ISMENE I did the deed, if she acknowledges it; I share the burden   500
of the charge.

ANTIGONE No! Justice will not allow you that; you refused, and
so I did not share the work.

ISMENE In your troubles I am not ashamed to make my own
voyage of suffering with you.   505

ANTIGONE Hades and the dead know whose act it was; I cannot
love someone who loves in word alone.

ISMENE Sister, do not deny me the right to die with you and to
honour the man who is dead.

ANTIGONE Do not share my death, and do not claim deeds you   510
never put your hand to; my death will suffice.

ISMENE What desire can I feel for life, abandoned by you?

ANTIGONE Ask Creon; he is the one you care for.

ISMENE Why do you hurt me when it does you no good?

ANTIGONE If I laugh at you, there is pain in my laughter.   515

ISMENE Then what can I do to help you now?

ANTIGONE Save yourself. I don't begrudge you your escape.

ISMENE Oh no! Am I to have no share in your fate?

ANTIGONE No. You chose to live, I to die.

521–2 some … others With whom does Antigone think (a) Ismene and (b) she herself found favour?

Antigone and Ismene

Creon acknowledges (526–7) that the two sisters are different in character. He would have approved of Ismene's cautious 'good sense' in lines 45–60 (the 'arguing' to which she refers in 520), but now Ismene is as 'mad' as Antigone. Ismene admits (528) that she is no longer acting rationally.

- How well does the dialogue of this passionate exchange (500–25) differentiate the two characters?
- Do we see a new side of Ismene?
- Is Antigone still as scornful and spiteful towards her sister? Are there signs of a more gentle tone (e.g. 515)?
- What do you think are Antigone's motives for refusing to let Ismene share in her suffering and fate? Is it for selfish or unselfish reasons?

Antigone's silence

Saying that she is already dead (524) – provoking a sneer from Creon (533) – Antigone remains silent for the rest of the scene (but see note on 538).

- Would you want to emphasise her silence? How?
- How does Antigone's growing isolation affect our attitude to her?
- What qualities does Ismene show in the exchange with Creon?

534 the woman betrothed to your own son This revelation that Antigone is betrothed to Haemon, Creon's son (not a traditional feature of the story), is a surprise. Ismene tries a new appeal, to Creon's own family feeling. Betrothal was usually arranged by the heads of families; the series of crises in the family may have made the match of cousins seem expedient, but Ismene implies (536) that the two love one another, and this impression is strengthened by events later in the play.

- Why do you think that Antigone has made no mention of her betrothal?

535 plough The phrase is as coarse in Greek as it is in English.

538 Dearest Haemon In all the manuscripts of the play this line is spoken by Ismene, but since the early sixteenth century there have been editors who have thought that it belongs to Antigone.

- How differently would we think of Antigone if it were she who uttered this solitary cry?

543 Creon starts to restore order by sending the women indoors, where they belong (see 15 and note on 489). We are to assume there will be a delay before the sisters are sent to their death.

ISMENE Not without my arguing against it.   520

ANTIGONE Your views found favour with some, and mine with
others.

ISMENE And yet we both share equal guilt!

ANTIGONE Be strong. You are alive, but my spirit died a long
time ago, to serve the dead.   525

CREON I declare that one of these two has just revealed she's mad,
the other has done so ever since her birth.

ISMENE That is true, lord. What sense we're born with does not
stay when disaster strikes; it deserts us.

CREON It did for you, when you chose to commit crimes with   530
criminals.

ISMENE How am I to live alone without her?

CREON She ... Don't speak of her. She no longer exists.

ISMENE So you will kill the woman betrothed to your own son?

CREON Yes. There are other fields for him to plough.   535

ISMENE But not the ties that bound him to her.

CREON I won't have criminal wives for my sons!

ISMENE Dearest Haemon, how your father wrongs you!

CREON You and your talk of marriage! You infuriate me!

ISMENE Will you really rob your own son of her?   540

CREON It is Hades who will end their marriage for me.

ISMENE So it seems decided that she will die.

CREON We are agreed. No more delay! Servants, take her inside.
From now on they must be women and not go wandering
outside. Even the bold try to escape when they see Hades   545
coming to end their lives.

SECOND CHORAL ODE (2ND *STASIMON*) (547–96)

The imminent fate of the sisters throws the Chorus into sombre reflection. They sing of the curse (*atē*) which can remorselessly destroy a family, generation by generation. Now the sisters, the last survivors of their clan, are destroyed by foolish infatuation. Zeus is invincible. No human crime or aggrandisement can escape punishment: god, through men's ambition and desire, controls their minds and leads them to destruction.

549 a house has been shaken by the gods The same Theban citizens, who in the first *stasimon* sang in almost humanist terms of man's position in the world, here turn to an ancient belief that the gods send ruin (*atē* 550, 580, 589, 590) to destroy whole families, usually to avenge some crime. (The idea is hinted at in the first sentence of the play, 1–3.) It could be visited on the victims in the form of infatuation (also *atē*), frenzy (569), hope (581), delusion (582) or dizzy-minded lusts (583) – and there was no release, generation after generation.

558 Labdacus' son Laius provoked the curse (see Background to the story, page vii). He and Oedipus' family are 'the house of Labdacus'.

564–9 the light ... Fury in the mind In this strange, mixed metaphor 'the light' is the two sisters, the last remaining chance of further life for the family, which has been cut off. Here it is the gods below who are responsible, working through Antigone's foolish words (the Chorus echo Creon's words 'she's mad', 526) and a frenzy in her mind. The imagery is highly wrought, and the details complex, but the overall sense is reasonably clear.

569 a Fury The Greek *Erinys*, a fiend or Fury, belongs in the dark, primitive world of retributive justice: a supernatural agent whose role was to ensure that a person received his or her rightful fate. Here the Fury is imagined to be a frenzy in Antigone's mind, driving her to her doom.

570 transgression Antigone has broken the law (Creon 416), but no such human transgression can shake Zeus' power. The Chorus now turn from the sphere of the gods below (Antigone's preoccupation) to the supreme deity of Olympus, Zeus the invincible, the ultimate guarantee that no human aggrandisement can prosper (see note on Zeus, page 10).

572 All-conquering sleep In *Iliad xiv* Sleep claims to be able to master all the gods except Zeus.

573 months of the gods The gods control the seasons, which rotate tirelessly. The Chorus stress that Zeus' power is eternal (576–7) and ageless (574).

CHORUS
Blessed are they whose life
Has tasted no evil.
When a house has been shaken by the gods,
The ruin never leaves them, but creeps on   550
Through generations of the family.
Like a surge from the open sea,
When the darkness of the deep
Is driven on by the angry winds of Thrace;
It rolls up black sand from the depths,   555
And windswept headlands roar and groan
As the waves strike against them.

I see that the sorrows of the house of Labdacus
Are age-old,
Piling on the sorrows of the dead;   560
One generation does not free the next,
But a god strikes them down,
And there is no escape.
Now the light that spread
Over the last roots of Oedipus' house,   565
Now it too is mown down
By the bloody scythe of the gods below,
By senseless words,
And a Fury in the mind.

Zeus, what human transgression   570
Can restrain your power?
All-conquering sleep cannot master it,
Nor the tireless months of the gods;
A king unaged by time,
You dwell in the marble radiance of Olympus.   575
This law holds fast tomorrow and forever,
As in the past.
But no mortal life
Climbs to the heights of power
Without disaster.   580

588 evil comes to seem good As in the first *stasimon*, the Chorus seem here (581–90) to go beyond the immediate situation of the play. They do not accuse Antigone of seeking inordinate power (579) or having dizzy lusts (583), but prompt us to reflect in general on the delusions which can drive mortals to their ruin. Their suggestion that people do not always anticipate the consequences of their actions (584–6) may hint at a sympathetic understanding of Antigone; and the audience may wonder if the Chorus' words in fact apply more to Creon than to Antigone. In contrast to Creon's certainties (482–3, 486) Antigone's piety seems less assertive (484–5).

592 The youngest of your sons was Haemon: the elder son Megareus was dead (see 1268).

- The Chorus set the conflict of the play in the context of Zeus' almighty power. How does this affect our view of the characters?
- How does the rich, involved imagery of this ode affect the mood of the play?

THIRD EPISODE (597–728)

Though we are not immediately aware of it, the ode covers a passage of time (see note on 645). Creon is next confronted by his son Haemon. Sometimes the speeches of an *agōn* are formal or highly structured; in this one (597–714), for example, Creon and Haemon have an equal number of lines.

599 raging in anger After Creon's outburst to the Chorus at 258–9 and to Ismene at 495–6, we are perhaps prepared for such a greeting. He used a similar word when he said that Ismene was 'hysterical' (450).

- We may wonder why Creon uses such language here: does he really expect Haemon to behave in this way? Is he being provocative? If so, why? Is it a further sign of his insecurity?

Haemon's first words

601 Father, I am yours The Chorus as well as Creon anticipated that Haemon would be in an emotional state; so his controlled and calmly submissive tone is a surprise. And because this is what Creon wants, it provokes the question: is Haemon being sincere or just tactful? He does not answer Creon's question, whether he has heard the verdict on Antigone.

- Do you think Haemon's behaviour suggests that he does know Antigone's fate? (There has been a passage of time – note on 645.)

Far-ranging hope is a comfort to many men,
But to many it is the delusion
Of dizzy-minded lusts.
It comes to the man who knows nothing
Until he puts his foot   585
In the heat of the fire.
From a man of wisdom came that famous saying
That evil comes to seem good to one
Whose mind a god leads to ruin.
The small man lives his life outside disaster.   590

But here is Haemon,
The youngest of your sons.
Does he come grieving
For the fate (of his destined wife),
Of his bride, Antigone,   595
Bitter for his broken hopes of marriage?

CREON We will soon know, better than prophets could tell us. My
son, have you heard the final verdict on your betrothed? Have
you come raging in anger against your father? Or do I still hold
your love whatever I do?   600

HAEMON Father, I am yours. You have good judgement, and the
orders you give me I shall follow. I shall value no marriage
more highly than your good guidance.

Fathers and sons

A father, as head of his household (*oikos* or *domos*), could renounce or disinherit his sons, who owed him total obedience. Creon hopes for unconditional devotion from Haemon (600). In the traditional morality of 'helping friends and harming enemies' (page 2), a son is expected to adopt his father's loyalties (607–8), to be a credit to his father (608–10), to look after him in old age and to guard his honour and reputation after death (e.g. Orestes' obligation to avenge his dead father, Agamemnon). It was a matter of honour that the *oikos* should not die out or be destroyed, and it was through his sons that a man perpetuated his *oikos*.

610 laughter For Creon's fear of mockery see note on page 36.

Creon's attitude to women

Creon, in his homily on the duties of a son, moves on to the choice of a wife (611–14). Love matches were rare in the classical world, and Creon's advice is not so remarkable as the language which he uses ('Spit her out' 615, see also 535). His coarse, offensive manner when he talks of sensitive and spiritual matters becomes increasingly obvious (see note on 489).

616 the only one There have been enough suggestions that there is opposition to Creon (see note on 462) for this remark to arouse doubts about his sense of realism. After his edict, it is a matter of personal honour for Creon not to let anyone see him go back on his word.

618 I will kill her Note the cold, curt phrase.

618–19 Zeus who protects the family Zeus, like other gods, had more than one function and in prayers it was customary to specify the role in which one sought his help. Creon's dismissive reference to Antigone's prayers to the god of the family (see notes on 447 and 570) borders on blasphemy.

● How does this colour our view of Creon's previous claims to reverence Zeus (see note on 277)?

623 give orders to his superiors Antigone has transgressed the law and – probably in Creon's eyes – tried to 'dictate to' her superiors (417–23).

623–5 These lines are thought to have been added after Sophocles' time. The reference to an elected leader suggests a more democratic state than Creon's Thebes, and breaks the sequence of thought.

628 a trustworthy comrade Soldiers in ancient Greece were not professionals; part of being a good citizen was being a good comrade in arms. Creon's recent involvement in the defence of Thebes makes this a natural concern of his. It is the male world which he understands.

CREON That, my son, is how you ought to feel in your heart; to
          stand by your father's judgement in all matters. For this reason   605
          men pray that the children they produce and keep in their
          house may be obedient, to do harm to their father's enemies,
          and honour his friends as he does. But the man who fathers
          useless sons – what could you say he has produced but troubles
          for himself, and a great stock of laughter for his enemies?   610
          My son, never abandon your good sense to pleasure, for a
          woman; remember that what you embrace turns cold in your
          arms, an evil woman sharing your bed and home. And what
          wounds more deeply than a loved one who is evil?
          Spit her out like an enemy, let this girl marry someone in   615
          Hades. Since I caught her here, the only one from the whole
          city openly to disobey me, I will not show myself false to my
          city; I will kill her. Let her sing hymns to Zeus who protects the
          family; for if I support relatives who are lawless, then truly I
          must do the same for others outside my family. Whoever is a   620
          good man in his house will be shown to be just in the city;
          whereas whoever transgresses and breaks the laws, or thinks to
          give orders to his superiors, can win no praise from me. (The
          man the city puts in charge must be listened to, in small things
          and in great, just and otherwise.) And I would be confident   625
          that this man would be both a good ruler and a willing subject;
          in the storm of spears he would remain where he was placed,
          a trustworthy comrade.

633–5 never be worsted by a woman Creon's view relates to Antigone, but is further evidence of his deep-seated misogyny (see also 444–5, 489, 611–14).

Creon on obedience (620–35)

For Creon, the same discipline and obedience that are important in the family are necessary in public life. The man who accepts others' rule, himself makes a good ruler and a valuable comrade. Obedience tends to success, disobedience to ruin. So obey the rules and (the sequence of thought is tenuous) don't give in to a woman. If you are going to lose power, lose it to a man.

- How effective is Creon's argument?
- How well does this speech complement his previous statements on government (168–80, 267–9, note on 469)?

Creon's language

Creon falls readily into broad generalisations and maxims (*gnōmai*). His words on obedience (629–32) have the same form and dogmatic tone as those on the evil of money (271–5), giving the impression of someone wanting to display assurance and wisdom. There are similar pronouncements on, for example, government (168–80), stubbornness (435–8), self-incrimination (451–2), hatred of enemies (482–3, 486) and good sons (605–10).

Haemon's reply

Haemon praises good sense, which Creon has urged him to follow (611). Having implied that he agrees with Creon (639–40), he tells him of the sympathy for Antigone which he hears in the city, confirming what Antigone herself said (467) of hidden support. Insisting that he wants only his father's well-being (651), he urges him not to be rigid, but to listen to advice. The eulogy of Antigone contained within the speech (646–50), which is carefully attributed to other citizens (645, 650), echoes her own language (460–1). We are encouraged to think that others feel as she does: that in burying 'her own brother' (647) she was indeed doing something 'glorious' (647).

645 under cover of darkness This implies a passage of time since Creon condemned Antigone to death.

655–8 seen to be empty Though Haemon speaks of a nameless man, we think of Creon, so that line 657 has the resonance of a prophecy.

But there is no worse evil than disobedience. It destroys cities, and leaves houses abandoned; it breaks and puts to flight the allied spear-ranks. For those who succeed, it is to obedience that they most owe their lives. So we must uphold the laws, and never be worsted by a woman. It is better, if one must fall from power, to fall to a man; then we would not be called inferior to women.   635

CHORUS Unless we have been robbed of our wits by time, you seem to us to speak with wisdom.

HAEMON Father, the gods plant wisdom in mankind, and it is the greatest of all our possessions. I cannot say that you are not right to speak as you do, and I would not know how. (And yet   640 it could be that another view is right.) It is not your nature to pay attention to everything that people say or do or find to criticise; and your look frightens the citizens and prevents them saying things you would not like to hear. But I can hear under cover of darkness how the city mourns for this girl; they   645 say that of all women she least deserves to die in disgrace for such glorious deeds. When her own brother lay unburied where he was killed, she did not allow him to be torn apart by scavenging dogs or birds; does she not deserve a golden prize of honour? That is the dark rumour that spreads in secret.   650 For me, father, there is nothing I value more than your success. What greater reward can children have than their father flourishing in glory, or he from them? Do not, then, keep one idea fixed in your mind, that what you say is right and nothing else. For the man who believes that he alone has the   655 ability to think and speak, that he and no-one else possesses intelligence – when such men are laid open, they are seen to be empty.

660–1 You see how the trees Haemon reinforces his advice to be flexible by repetition of one Greek verb (*eikein*, 'bend' 661, 'slacken' 664, 'let [...] go' 666). When the Chorus said that Antigone did not know how to yield (*eikein*), Creon was confident she could be broken (435–8).

● Contrast Creon's language (435–8) with Haemon's here (660–5).

666 anger The word helps us to see how Creon appears to Haemon.
○ Explore ways of presenting Creon's anger in his long speech (604–35).

The Chorus
The Chorus, with customary diplomacy, commend both speeches (636–7, 670–1, see note on page 34). But significantly they endorse Haemon's words (659–60, 670–1), that it is good to listen to advice.

Stichomythia
After their extended speeches the two characters are involved in an exchange of one and two lines, which builds to a highly dramatic and bitter climax (673–714).

Creon's intolerance

673 are men of my age to be taught... Creon's incredulous, indignant tone, totally dismissing Haemon's (666, 669) and the Chorus' (670–1) cautious advice, reminds us of a previous outburst to the Chorus (258–9): then the Chorus were too old to give advice; here Haemon is too young!

678 the disease is presumably that of 'honouring traitors'.

679 united people of Thebes This suggestion that not only is there an opinion other than Creon's (see 655–7), but that the state is united against Creon, provokes him to an even greater fury.

Creon's tyranny exposed
Creon's insistence on autocratic power (680–4) explains the Chorus' cautious compliance (197), and confirms Antigone's view of the nature of his rule (462–3). Haemon (683) voices the view of most Greeks that the word 'state/city' (*polis*) entailed the citizens' involvement to at least some degree in the institutions of government. Creon's apparent belief that the city belongs to its ruler (684) is essentially the view that 'Might is Right' (see note on page 6). Haemon's fearless refusal to be cowed by his father exposes once and for all Creon's unsuitability to rule (685). Creon is reduced to indignant questions (673, 676, 680, 682, 684, 688, 690), insults (693, 707) and threats (698, 703, 709–10).

● What light does this scene throw on the views of government which Creon expressed on his first entry (168–80)?

No, however intelligent a man may be, it is no disgrace for him
to learn still more, and not to be too inflexible. You see how   660
the trees that bend beside the storming winter floods save even
their twigs, while those that resist are torn up by their roots;
and so too the man who hauls tight the mainsheet of his sail
and will not slacken it capsizes his ship and ends the voyage
with the rowing benches upside down.   665
Let your anger go, and allow change. If I may offer an opinion,
young as I am, I say that it would be best for man to be born
perfect in wisdom; otherwise – and it does not tend to turn out
so – it is good to learn from those whose words are wise.

CHORUS My lord, if what he says is timely, it is right that you   670
learn from him – and for you, Haemon, to learn from your
father; for you have both spoken well.

CREON So are men of my age to be taught sense by a man of his?

HAEMON In nothing that is not right. If I am young, judge not
my age, but rather what I do.   675

CREON And what you do is honour those who break the law?

HAEMON I would not tell you to honour traitors.

CREON Is that not the disease that has infected her?

HAEMON The united people of Thebes say not.

CREON Will the city tell me how I must rule?   680

681 As though *you* were the child! Creon has claimed superiority on the grounds of his age (673).

686 This man, it seems Creon addresses the Chorus, whom he seems to be trying to bring into the debate.
● What might this suggest?

687 If you are a woman! Why are these words particularly provocative?

688 You worthless boy!
● Is Creon listening to Haemon? Or overwhelmed with indignation that he argues with his father?

691–2 the gods' honour Creon rules by the grace of the gods, so he abuses his authority when he uses it to infringe the honour of the gods.

693 lower than a woman! Haemon's words (691–2) are too close an echo of Antigone's (419–21) for Creon. Haemon's apparent support for a woman is to Creon the ultimate shock and betrayal (see 686, 707).

694 The connection of thought is 'You may think me lower than a woman, but…'

695 To Creon 'every word' Haemon speaks is a 'shameful deed'.

698 marry her while she lives As at line 686 Creon abruptly changes tack, this time with a threat which recalls his sarcastic remarks of 488–9, 615–16.

699–700 she will destroy another Is it clear whom Haemon means?

707 humour Creon is probably referring to the manner in which Haemon spoke the previous line.

708 You want to … hear nothing Though the argument has degenerated to mutual accusations of having no sense (703–6), Haemon is still talking to the point. But his implication that there should be some equality in the debate flouts Creon's notion of a son's dutiful behaviour.

709 By Olympus Creon is almost dumbfounded. In oaths Olympus is the sky, as in our 'By Heavens!'
● In what sense could Creon's response (709–11) be said to encompass all his weaknesses?

710 Bring out The attendants (see note on 450) bring Antigone at line 750.
● What does Creon intend to do? Is he going to kill her on the spot, but diverted by Haemon's exit and the Chorus' anxious question (719)?

HAEMON You see how you speak? As though *you* were the child!

CREON Should I rule this land for others than myself?

HAEMON It is no city at all that belongs to one man.

CREON Does the city not belong to its ruler, by law?

HAEMON You'd make a good king of an empty country. 685

CREON This man, it seems, is fighting on the woman's side.

HAEMON If you are a woman! My concern is for *you*.

CREON You worthless boy! Will you argue with your father?

HAEMON Yes, because I see you mistaken about what is just.

CREON So I am mistaken to respect the power I wield? 690

HAEMON Yes. You do not respect it when you trample on the gods' honour.

CREON You foul creature, lower than a woman!

HAEMON You will never find me giving way to shameful deeds.

CREON Every word you speak is spoken for that girl. 695

HAEMON And for you, and for me, and for the gods beneath the earth!

CREON There is no way you will ever marry her while she lives.

HAEMON So she will die; and in her death she will destroy another. 700

CREON Are you so far gone in recklessness to make threats?

HAEMON How is it a threat to speak my mind to you?

CREON You will regret your lecturing; you yourself don't talk sense.

HAEMON If you were not my father, I would say that you were 705
talking nonsense.

CREON Slave of a woman, don't try to humour me!

HAEMON You want to speak and hear nothing in reply?

CREON Can this be true? By Olympus, you can be sure you will
regret your taunts and insults! Bring out that hateful thing, so 710
she can die right now before her bridegroom's eyes!

714 friends The Greek word (*philoi*) includes relatives (page 2).

Creon's two changes of mind
Creon decides to spare Ismene (720).
● Why do you think this is?
Then, though the proclamation had prescribed death by stoning
(29–30), he decides to put Antigone in an excavated chamber (not a
natural cave – possibly a disused tomb: see 1167). Perhaps Haemon's
warnings about the feelings of the people have affected him after all;
perhaps he has had some religious compunction.

Burial alive
All killing entailed pollution (*miasma*), which could affect a whole
community (page 14), and which could be cleansed only by ritual
purification. Creon hopes to spare the city the guilt of responsibility
for Antigone's death by leaving some food: thus her death would be
due to 'natural causes'. Similarly in Sophocles' play *Philoctetes* the
Greeks who abandoned Philoctetes on a deserted island left him
scraps of food.

725–6 the only one of the gods she worships Creon does not
understand why Antigone is not as concerned as he about the gods of
Thebes whose temples Polyneices would have sacked. Antigone has
upheld, in the case of Polyneices' burial, the respect due to Hades, the
god of the underworld; this does not mean that she denies the divinity
of the Olympian gods. For Creon's scathing dismissal of Antigone's
piety (727) see also 618.

Creon and Haemon
● What picture of Haemon do we get from this scene?
● Is his first concern his father's welfare?
● What do we learn of his feelings for Antigone?
● Haemon begins the scene in a controlled and measured way, but
  leaves in anger (715). Where does he begin to lose control and
  reveal his emotions?
● How has our understanding of Creon developed?
● How does this scene resemble, and differ from, the first scene
  between Antigone and Ismene?
○ Is the formal structure in the two main speeches of this *agōn* a help
  or hindrance in performance?
○ Explore the dynamics of the scene. Are there 'climaxes'?

HAEMON No, she will not die in my presence; don't even imagine it. Nor will you ever set eyes on my face again; so you can rave on, with any of your friends who can endure it!

CHORUS The man has gone, my lord, with the speed of his anger. 715
The mind at his age takes it hard when hurt.

CREON Let him go; let him do or think what he likes – beyond mortal power. He will not save these girls from death.

CHORUS Do you really intend to kill them both?

CREON Not the one who did not touch him; you are right. 720

CHORUS But how do you plan to kill the other?

CREON I will take her to a place where men's feet have trodden no path, and I will bury her alive in a chamber of rock, giving her just enough food to avoid guilt, so that the city as a whole escapes pollution. There, praying to Hades, the only one of the 725 gods she worships, perhaps she will manage to avoid death; or she will learn, although too late, that worshipping the dead is wasted labour.

THIRD CHORAL ODE (3RD *STASIMON*) (729–57)

In the second ode the Chorus, seeking to explain the fate of Antigone and Ismene, explored the idea of an ancestral curse. Here they ascribe the cause of Haemon's quarrel with Creon to *Erōs*, the god of sexual desire, whom neither gods nor mortals can resist.

Love (*Erōs*)

Eros (Cupid) was originally an independent god of love; in later mythology he was the attendant or son of Aphrodite (Venus). But the two names are often interchangeable: with their arrows both could compel a person to fall in love. Eros/Aphrodite represents a fundamental force, beyond our control, which governs our lives – one of the mighty 'laws' (*thesmoi* 747), influencing our behaviour, like those which Antigone (421) will not transgress. Here, as elsewhere in Greek literature, this personification of sex is seen as destructive (see Euripides' plays, *Medea* and *Hippolytus*), capriciously (749) and violently driving its victims to madness, injustice and disgrace (739–40).

The Chorus say that Haemon's reason for opposing his father is *Erōs*. It will be easier to assess this later in the play, but at this stage:

● On what evidence do you think they base this opinion?
● If true, does it influence our view of Haemon's behaviour and arguments in the previous scene?

729–30 battle … rout wealth Love's activity is presented throughout the ode in military terms. It causes havoc in men's and women's lives, and so sometimes destroys fortunes.

733 dwellings of the country wilds The meaning is that love's influence is everywhere, no matter how humble or remote.

751 carried beyond laws (*thesmoi*) The sense is not clear. The Chorus may mean that pity tempts them too to rebel against Creon's laws (but this is awkward as *thesmoi* meant non-human laws in 747); or that in weeping they too, like Haemon, are succumbing to an irrational force.

756 chamber The Greek word (*thalamos*) is often used for the *bridal* chamber.

CHORUS Love, unconquered in battle,
        Love, you who rout wealth,   730
    Who keep watch on the soft cheeks of a girl,
        Who wander over the ocean
    And through dwellings of the country wilds.
        There is no escape from you,
            Neither for immortals,   735
            Nor for humans
            Whose life is for a day;
        And he who feels you is mad.

    You wrench the minds even of the just
            To injustice and outrage.   740
        You it is who have stirred up
    This strife between men of one blood.
            The bright desire
        In the eyes of the fair bride
            Has won the victory,   745
        Enthroned in power
        Beside the mightiest laws.
    For the goddess Aphrodite is unconquerable
        When she plays her games.

            But now I too   750
        Am carried beyond laws
            As I see this:
        I can no longer hold back
        The stream of my tears
        As I see this girl, Antigone,   755
        Making her way to the chamber
        Where all are laid to rest.

FOURTH EPISODE (758–908)

First *kommos*

Antigone is brought on, having been told her fate (759), and reflects on her situation, first (758–853), in a sung dialogue (*kommos*) with the Chorus, a feature of tragedy at moments of emotional intensity.

763 Acheron was one of the rivers of Hades.

765 hymns of my marriage Though she does not mention Haemon, Antigone draws attention to the pathos of dying unmarried. In the ceremony of marriage the bride was led in procession, to the accompaniment of a hymn to Hymen, the god of marriage, to the groom's home, and there another song (766) was sung outside the bridal chamber.

767 I will marry Acheron The pitiful words ironically echo Creon's bitter jibes (488, 615–16).

768 glorious Antigone has appeared to want glory (460). The Chorus try tentatively to console her with the thought that the unique aspects of her death – that she willed it (772) and that she will have a sort of living burial – will give her posthumous fame.

Niobe

It is not uncommon in Greek plays for characters or the Chorus to try to find a parallel in history or myth for the situation of the protagonist. 'Our Phrygian guest' (775) was Niobe, daughter of Tantalus, a king in Asia Minor (here called 'Phrygia'). Married to Amphion, the Theban king, she boasted that she had more children than the goddess Leto; at which Leto's two children, Apollo and Artemis, killed all her children. Niobe returned to Asia Minor, where she was turned to stone on Mount Sipylus; this rock face, over which waters streamed, was thought to be her petrified body. Antigone sees a resemblance to Niobe, in that her fate too began when she was still alive, imprisoned in a tomb of rock.

- Explore the complex details of the imagery. How effective do you find the simile?
- What does it tell us of Antigone's emotional state?

786 Fate (the Greek is *daimōn*, a divine spirit) The Greeks regularly attribute events outside their control to a god. This does not, however, imply that Antigone is attributing responsibility for her death to anyone but herself or denying that she chose it.

ANTIGONE   Look upon me, citizens of my fatherland,
                      Going on my last journey,
                  Looking at the sun for the last time,   760
                      As I never will again.
    Hades who puts all to sleep is leading me, still alive,
                  To the shores of Acheron.
                      I have had no share
              In the hymns of my marriage procession,   765
                  No wedding song has hymned me.
                      I will marry Acheron.

CHORUS   Do you not depart glorious and with praise
                  To that deep place of the dead?
                  Not stricken by wasting disease   770
              Not receiving the punishment of swords,
                      But by your own will,
                  Alone of mankind, while still alive,
                      You will go down to Hades.

ANTIGONE   I have heard how our Phrygian guest,   775
                  The daughter of Tantalus,
        Most pitifully died on the summit of Sipylus;
                  How, like strangling ivy,
              The growing stone overpowered her,
                  And the rains and the snow,   780
                      So men say,
                      Give her no respite
                      But wear her away,
              As below her ever-weeping brow
                  They pour down her sloping sides.   785
                      Fate puts me to sleep
                      Just like her.

790 Yet for a dying woman The Chorus question Antigone's likening herself to Niobe, because Niobe was of divine descent – her father was the son of Zeus. They are warning her against *hubris*. Yet, they say, it is still glorious for a mortal to have the fate of one who is god*like*.

793 In life and … in death Antigone has *not* resembled Niobe in her life. The insistence of the idea of 'living' seems to perpetuate the paradox of the 'living death' which Antigone faces (762, 773).

794 I am mocked! The idea of glory, which Antigone had talked of wanting (460), does not console her: when she identified her fate with Niobe's, it was the Chorus' pity which she was seeking. Creon too was afraid of mockery (see 610 and note on page 36).

800 Dirce See note on 95.

801 holy ground All Thebes is said to be a sanctuary, presumably because much of it was associated in legend with gods.

802 chariots See note on 144.

803 witnesses Antigone is anxious that her fate should not go unremarked (also 758).

804 unwept The Chorus said they wept (754), but the tears she craves are those of her loved ones (*philoi*). She is to be denied the very honours due to the dead which she was so determined to give her brother (see page 4).

809 With no home Antigone's sense that she is rejected by the city (*polis* 798) is accentuated by her use of the word *metoikos*, which described a (non-citizen) alien resident in a state (also 832, 859).

814 high throne of Justice Antigone claimed to uphold the Justice who 'dwells with the gods below' (418). The Chorus again see her, in challenging the justice of the state, as the victim of her father's sin (558–69).

Jane Lapotaire as Antigone with the Chorus, National Theatre production, London, 1984.

CHORUS   But she was a goddess, and born of gods,
While we are mortal and of mortal birth.
Yet for a dying woman,   790
It is a great thing even to hear
That she has won the destiny of the godlike
In life and afterwards in death.

ANTIGONE   Ah, I am mocked!
Why, by the gods of our fathers,   795
Can you not insult me when I have gone,
Instead of to my face?
Oh city,
Oh richly endowed sons of the city!
Oh springs of Dirce,   800
And holy ground of Thebes,
Where the chariots gather,
At least I have you as my witnesses:
How I go unwept by loved ones,
And with what ceremony,   805
To the newly raised mound
Of my strange tomb.
Oh ill-fated woman,
With no home among mortals
Nor as a corpse among corpses,   810
Neither with the living,
Nor with the dead.

CHORUS   You went to the extremity of daring,
To the high throne of Justice,
My child,   815
And you fell.
Your ordeal is payment
For your father.

820 most agonising thought The Chorus' words cause Antigone to reflect again (see 1–5) on the family curse. In her emotional turmoil she sees herself as doomed by the incestuous marriage of her parents (47–8, 824–7) and Polyneices' marriage (835) – doomed to be denied marriage herself.

821 thrice-told doom She means 'often repeated' fate.

● How important has the thought that she is Oedipus' daughter been to Antigone?

833 my brother Not an oblique reference to her father, with whom she shared a mother, but to Polyneices, whose marriage to the Argive princess, Argeia, sealed his alliance with Argos and led to his attack on Thebes.

The attitude of the Chorus

The Chorus have tried to show some sympathy, to find consolation for Antigone, to reconcile her to her fate, but without being able to comprehend her motives. They resort to two explanations: (a) the family curse (817) and (b) Antigone's 'daring' (813) and her 'self-willed temper' (841). The Greeks found it possible to set events in the context of supernatural influences, while at the same time believing that humans must accept responsibility for their actions (see note on 786). The Chorus are quite clear that Antigone is at fault, because she defied the authority of the ruler (813–16, 838–40).

Antigone

The isolation which Antigone has so boldly braved now unnerves her. She laments her family doom and her lonely plight, unmarried and without her loved ones to mourn her death (see 804, 844, 852). The thought that she will die unmarried seems particularly oppressive and provokes thoughts of the disastrous marriages in her family (824, 835).

● How much is she affected by the response of the Chorus?

● How convincing do you find her change from heroic defiance to self-pity?

○ In performance would you have Creon listen to the whole exchange between the Chorus and Antigone (see 854)? If so, do you think the Chorus should be shown to be affected by his presence?

ANTIGONE	You have touched on
	My most agonising thought,	820
	The thrice-told doom of my father,
	The entire destiny that has come to us,
	To the famous children of Labdacus.
	Alas for the horrors of my mother's bed!
	My doomed mother	825
	Lying with her own son,
	My father!
	From what parents
	Was I then born for misery!
	To them I go,	830
	Accursed and unmarried,
	To share their home.
	Alas, my brother,
	Who made
	Such an ill-fated marriage!	835
	In your death you have destroyed me
	Even as I live.

ANTIGONE   You have touched on
           My most agonising thought,   820
      The thrice-told doom of my father,
    The entire destiny that has come to us,
    To the famous children of Labdacus.
  Alas for the horrors of my mother's bed!
         My doomed mother   825
       Lying with her own son,
           My father!
         From what parents
      Was I then born for misery!
          To them I go,   830
       Accursed and unmarried,
         To share their home.
         Alas, my brother,
           Who made
       Such an ill-fated marriage!   835
  In your death you have destroyed me
          Even as I live.

CHORUS   Reverent action is a kind of piety,
    But the man in whom power resides
    Cannot let his power be infringed.   840
      Your self-willed temper
        Has destroyed you.

ANTIGONE   Unmourned,
       Without loved ones,
     Without my marriage-song,   845
       I am led in misery
    On the journey that is prepared.
    No longer do I have the right
  To see this sacred light of the sun,
        Wretched as I am.   850
       My fate is unwept,
       And no loved one
        Mourns for me.

Creon

Creon is completely unaffected by Antigone's grief. Note his curt language (855–7). His conscience seems clear (858, see note on page 56).

- Antigone clearly cannot '*live* entombed' (858). What does Creon's remark suggest about his mental state?

861 my bridal chamber The idea of marriage in death recurs (see 767).

863 Persephone was the daughter of Demeter, seized by Hades, the ruler of the underworld, to be his consort.

865 I nurse the hope Greek notions of an afterlife were vague, but Antigone finds consolation in the thought of being reunited with her family, who, if anyone, should acknowledge her worth.

867 dear brother Antigone seems to be thinking of Eteocles, though her words at line 20 implied that she was not present at his funeral.

Antigone's reasoning

Hitherto Antigone has given the impression that the burial of Polyneices was an unquestionable duty which was owed to all relatives; she presented it as a universal law of the gods below (417–26). Yet in lines 871–80 she says not only that she would not have done it for a husband or child; but also that she buried Polyneices only because (their parents being dead) as a brother he was irreplaceable. Many scholars have suspected that the lines were not written by Sophocles, but added later, possibly by actors. They argue:

(a) The ideas are borrowed from a story told by the historian Herodotus, a contemporary of Sophocles, in which a captive of the Persian king Darius is allowed to choose one relative to spare from slaughter and chooses her brother, for the reasons which Antigone gives.

(b) The argument is an unconvincing and bizarre way for Antigone to justify sacrificing her life.

(c) The speech seems dramatically inept and confuses our perception of Antigone's motivation.

Against these points it may be argued:

(a) The passage was familiar to Aristotle, who lived only two generations after Sophocles.

(b) Just as at 417–32 Antigone rationalised what was an instinctive act of devotion to her brother, so here she seeks further rational explanations of her behaviour; the speech, complementing the emotional *kommos*, offers a more reasoned exploration of her mind.

(c) The lack of logic is evidence of the pressure which she is under.

- Examine the structure and language of the speech. Do they suggest that Antigone is incoherent and confused?
- How does the speech, as it stands, affect your response to Antigone?
- Do you find it plausible that Antigone should speak in this way?

CREON Do you not realise that no-one would cease pouring out songs and lamentations before his death, if it could help? Lead her away at once, shut her in the covered tomb, as I proclaimed, and leave her alone, deserted, whether she wishes to die, or to live, entombed in such a home. I am guiltless regarding this girl; but she will lose her rights to live in the world above.

ANTIGONE My tomb, my bridal chamber, my grave and home that will guard me forever, where I go to meet my own, the great number of dead that Persephone has received. The last of these to pass below is myself, most wretchedly by far, before the span of my life has elapsed. And yet I nurse the hope that my father will welcome me with love; that I will be loved by you, my mother, and by you, dear brother; for when you died, with my own hands I washed and dressed you, and poured libations on your graves. But now, Polyneices, for tending your body, I have won this reward.

And yet I was right to honour you, as the wise will agree. If I were a mother, and my children were rotting in death, or my husband, I would never have taken on this task against the city's will. What law do I respect in saying this? I could have had another husband if one had died, and a child from another man, if I had lost one; but with my mother and father hidden in Hades, no other brother to me could be born. It was by this law that I gave you special honour; but to Creon I seem to have committed a crime, to have acted with outrageous daring, my dear brother.

Antigone's final home

Antigone is not to have the fulfilment of her womanhood, to be led by her father in her marriage procession from the family home to that of her groom (note on 765). She will miss the excitement and the celebration of the wedding (766, 845); she must sacrifice her sexual and maternal role (881–3), consoling herself with the thought of reunion with her family (865–7). She will be led by Hades (762, 846) to her new, final home, which she conceives both as a bridal chamber (861) and as a place where she will hope to find again the security of the family home.

885 What justice Antigone's plaintive question falls on deaf ears: the laws which she respects derive from the justice of the gods below (418); the justice of Creon and the Chorus (814) is that of the state.

890 these people Antigone does not refer to Creon by name.

891 I pray they suffer no more
- Is she being magnanimous?
- What is Antigone's tone at the end of her speech?

Creon

Creon ordered the guards to remove Antigone at line 856; even now there is further delay.
- How would you show Creon relating to the emotional intensity of the scene?
- Would you explain the delay by saying there is an element of non-naturalism in Greek tragedies, that the action can be 'frozen'?

Antigone's exit

Antigone rouses herself for a proud and defiant farewell (900–8), before being led out. It is as a royal princess that she takes her leave, and there is a hint of reproach to the 'Lords of Thebes' that they abandon her. Her disdain for Ismene is undiminished: she sees herself as the last of her family (863, 905); for her Ismene does not exist. In her last words she asserts her conviction that she is dying for a just, religious cause.
- Have your sympathies for Antigone been changed by the scene (758–908)?
- Do you think our view of her is different from that of an ancient audience?

And now he is having me seized and led away, unmarried, with
no wedding song, without my share in marriage and the
raising of children. So, bereft of loved ones and wretched in
my fate, I go alive to the graves of the dead.

What justice of the gods have I transgressed? Why should I   885
look to the gods any longer in my misfortune? What ally
should I call upon? For in acting with reverence I have earned
the charge of irreverence.

But if this is fair in the gods' eyes, when I have suffered I will
understand that I have sinned. But if it is these people who are   890
the sinners, I pray they suffer no more than they wrongfully
inflict on me.

CHORUS   Still the same storms,
                       These blasts of the soul
                       Have this girl in their power.   895

CREON   For this her escort will regret their slowness.

ANTIGONE   Ah, that word comes very close to death!

CREON   I cannot encourage you to hope:
                  The sentence will be carried out.

ANTIGONE   City of my fathers in the land of Thebes,   900
                   And our ancestral gods,
                        I am led away,
                    And I delay no longer.
                 Lords of Thebes, look upon me,
                   The sole surviving daughter   905
                      Of the royal house.
            See what I suffer, and at whose hands,
                Because I respected reverence.

FOURTH CHORAL ODE (4TH *STASIMON*) (909–61)

The ode is made up of three stories from myth, which illustrate the power of fate and in various (though not transparent) ways relate to Antigone.

Danae

Acrisius, king of Argos, was told by the oracle at Delphi that he would be killed by his daughter's son. To prevent her conceiving, he shut her in a bronze chamber. But Zeus entered her in a shower of golden rain and she became the mother of Perseus. Acrisius set the pair adrift in a chest, but Zeus rescued them and later Perseus accidentally killed Acrisius.

Lycurgus

Lycurgus, son of the king of the Thracian Edonians, tried – like Pentheus in Thebes (see Euripides' *Bacchae*) – to resist the spread of the cult of Bacchus (Dionysus) (see note on page 84). The god imprisoned him and he was later torn to pieces by wild horses.

Cleopatra

Cleopatra, daughter of the wind god Boreas and the Athenian princess Oreithyia, married Phineus, king of Salmydessus in Thrace. But when she had borne him two sons, he locked her away (this detail is not in all versions of the story) and took another wife, who savagely blinded the two boys and imprisoned them.

The significance of the ode

The theme of the third *stasimon* was that no-one can avoid the power of Eros. Here it is destiny that is inescapable. The Chorus seem to be trying to provide pointers as to the ways in which the audience might react to Antigone's situation. The traditional myths offered a body of familiar stories, to which it was natural for the Greeks to refer (as Antigone compared herself to Niobe, 775).

The first story is of an innocent princess imprisoned. The second is of a violent man who in time came to recognise the error of actions into which his rage had led him. The Chorus has in fact blamed Antigone for her rage (841) and she herself said that she may come to recognise the error of her action (889–90). But Antigone is not, as Lycurgus was, guilty of impiety.

The final section, to which most space is given, claims to show that even an innocent semi-divine princess, brought up in the wild, elemental caves of the north wind, could not avoid her destined fate (960–1). But she is not mentioned by name, it is not even a regular feature of the story that she was imprisoned, and the emphasis is on the fate of her sons, blinded by their savage stepmother.

CHORUS   Lovely Danae too endured this fate:
                Exchanging the light of heaven   910
                   For bronze-bound halls;
                She was kept prisoner, hidden away
                   In a chamber like a tomb.
                And yet she too was from a noble family,
                   My child, my child,   915
                And she nurtured the seed of Zeus
                   That fell in golden rain.
                But the power of fate is awesome;
                   Nothing can escape it,
                Not wealth, nor war, no fortress,   920
                Nor black ships beaten by the sea.

                The sharp-tempered son of Dryas,
                   King of the Edonians,
                   Was also imprisoned;
                For his frenzied taunting   925
                He was confined by Dionysus
                   In a prison of rock.
                So the terrible flowering of his rage
                   Drained away;
                He came to know that in his madness,   930
                   With his mocking words,
                   He had attacked a god.
                   He had tried to restrain
                   The god-possessed women,
                   And the fire of Dionysus;   935
                   And he enraged the Muses
                Who love the music of the pipe.

The Chorus of Theban elders have shown little independent or objective judgement. Here maybe they reveal how hard it is for men like them to fit Antigone's situation into any familiar pattern of reference. Choruses, like characters in plays, are not omniscient. They can be mistaken; and sometimes their lack of understanding can be ironic, offering unintentional significance. It has, for example, been suggested that the first two stories, in the characters of Acrisius and Lycurgus, have more relevance to Creon than to Antigone and obliquely prefigure his fate.

937 the pipe The *aulos* was a wind instrument, a sort of double-reed pipe; it was used to accompany the odes in tragedy.

938 dark sea rocks The Bosporus, the straits between the Black Sea and the Aegean, was flanked by huge rocks, alleged to clash and threaten passing ships. See map on page ix.

942–3 Ares … Saw the … wound Ares (see note on 116), the natural patron of the warlike Thracians, seems to have looked on with pleasure at the blinding.

947 the shuttle Women spent a lot of time weaving, and the shuttle made a natural weapon.

954 the ancient Erechtheidae are the Athenians, the sons of Erechtheus, the mythical founder of Athens. His temple, the Erechtheum, built after *Antigone* was first performed, still stands on the Acropolis. Cleopatra's mother Oreithyia was his daughter.

The ode

We cannot know how a Greek audience would have reacted to this difficult and complex ode; or how much its effectiveness depended on knowledge of details of the stories – not included here. The safest approach for us is to focus on the details to which Sophocles has given prominence.

- What ideas and images stand out?
- How do you think they relate to the dramatic context and the attitude of the Chorus? Do they put Antigone's courage and achievement into some sort of perspective?
- Does the ode add to our understanding of Antigone? Heighten the tension? Deepen the mood of impending doom? Provide a lull for reflection?
- What would you want the ode to contribute to the audience's appreciation of the play in performance?
- How might distribution of lines among individuals or groups help to clarify the ode's significance?
- What sort of music would be appropriate?

By the dark sea rocks,
By the waters of the double sea,
Are the shores of the Bosporus,   940
And Thracian Salmydessus;
Where Ares, protector of the city,
Saw the cursed, blinding wound
Inflicted on the two sons of Phineus
By his savage wife,   945
Bringing darkness to those eyes craving vengeance,
Stabbed by the point of the shuttle
In her bloodstained hands.

Pining away in misery,
They wept for their wretched fate,   950
Born to a mother
Unlucky in her marriage.
She was a queen
From the seed of the ancient Erechtheidae;
In faraway caves she was reared   955
In her father's storms,
The child of Boreas,
Swift as a horse over steep mountains,
The daughter of gods;
But even over her, my child,   960
The immortal Fates held sway.

FIFTH EPISODE (962–1074)

We have seen Creon in confrontation with Antigone, Ismene and Haemon. Each of them brought different arguments to bear against him. Now a new character appears, with a more formidable authority.

Teiresias

Teiresias, the old Theban seer, appears in many tragedies. Though blind, he can 'see' beyond mortal knowledge and he provides a kind of objective truth within the conflict of the drama. His special science is augury (divination based on observation of birds); the behaviour of birds offered signs or omens by which, with the help of his assistant, he could judge whether the gods approved of human actions or plans.

967 in the past Note that Creon has hitherto – presumably when regent for the two young princes – valued Teiresias' guidance (969) and earned his approval. His concern at the tone of Teiresias' voice (971) shows his continued respect.

977 quite clear The fact that the birds' cries were unintelligible is in itself an omen.

The sacrifice

Teiresias tries another form of divination (978): the way in which the sacrificial offering (sheep's thigh bones, covered with fat, and some of the intestines) burned, and the form of the flame, would reveal to him the attitude of the gods. That it failed to burn is both a symbolic sign of the gods' disapproval (987–9) and evidence of the physical pollution, caused by birds carrying about Polyneices' dead flesh (985–7).

Teiresias and Creon, Lincoln Center Repertory production, New York.

TEIRESIAS Lords of Thebes, we have come sharing our journey, two seeing through the eyes of one; this is how the blind must go, with a guide.

CREON What is the news, old Teiresias? 965

TEIRESIAS I will tell you, and you must obey the seer.

CREON I have not rejected your advice in the past.

TEIRESIAS And so you have steered the city well.

CREON From my experience I can bear witness to your help.

TEIRESIAS Know that you are walking on the razor edge of fate. 970

CREON What is it? How I shudder at your words!

TEIRESIAS You will know, when you hear the evidence of my art. As I sat on my ancient seat of augury, where every kind of bird finds a haven, I heard a strange cry from the birds, screeching with a terrible, incomprehensible frenzy. I realised that they 975 were tearing one another with murderous talons; for the flapping of their wings made that quite clear.

In fear I at once tried burning offerings on blazing altars; but the god of fire did not glow from the sacrifice. An oozing moisture dripped from the thigh-pieces onto the embers, and 980 smoked and spat; the gall was spattered into the air, and the melting thighs lay bare of the fat that had covered them. This I learned from the boy here, that my augury had failed, and that my rites gave no answers; for he is my guide, as I am guide to others. And it is through your decision that the city is sick. Our 985 altars and all our hearths are polluted with the carrion of birds and dogs, from that ill-fated fallen son of Oedipus. So the gods no longer accept prayer and sacrifice from us, nor the flame of roasted thigh-pieces, nor does any bird shriek a cry that we can understand, now they have fed on the fat of a dead man's 990 blood.

So think about this, my son. Mistakes are common to all men; but when a man makes a mistake, he is not foolish or doomed to failure if, after falling into trouble, he finds the remedy, instead of remaining obdurate. Stubbornness brings the charge 995 of stupidity.

Teiresias' advice

Teiresias, in urging Creon to yield (997), uses the same verb (*eikein*) as Haemon (see note on 660–1).

- In what way does Teiresias' advice to Creon resemble – and differ from – Haemon's (638–69)?
- How would you describe Teiresias' manner and tone towards Creon?
- Why do you think Teiresias does not mention Antigone? What is the effect of this?

1002 you all shoot

- What does this immediate response of Creon's suggest about his state of mind?

Creon's imagery

1004 trafficked Creon's imagery comes from the male world of commerce (1004–6, 1030, frequent references to 'profit'), war (627, 630–1, 1002), sailing (159–60, 179), the forge (436), the country (535) and the animal world (268, 438, 495).

1004–5 Take your profit Teiresias tried to assure Creon that his advice was for his (Creon's) advantage (1001). The Greek word (*kerdos*) can also mean financial 'profit', the motive which Creon attributes to those by whom he feels threatened (205, 270, 299). Now even Teiresias incurs the same charge (1012) in Creon's spiteful rejoinder.

1005 silver-gold was a natural alloy of silver and (predominantly) gold, found on the Tmolus mountain range near Sardis in Lydia (see map, page ix).

1006 gold of India India was hardly known to the Greeks of Sophocles' day, but through travellers' tales was thought to be fabulously rich.

1007 the eagles of Zeus As the king of birds, the eagle was naturally Zeus' favourite.

Blasphemy?

1009–10 no human has the power to defile the gods In a limited, literal sense Creon is right: mere mortals cannot inflict a *miasma* on immortals. But they can pollute, as Teiresias has shown, the altars of the gods, and Creon's hyperbolic image of eagles polluting Zeus' throne is shocking in its reckless blasphemy (see also note on 618–19).

1021–2 The whole breed of seers ... the race of tyrants...

- How do you react to this seemingly petulant tit-for-tat?

Yield to the dead man; do not stab him when he has fallen. What valour is there in killing the dead again? With good will towards you I give you good advice. Nothing is sweeter than learning from one who speaks well, if he speaks to your advantage.

CREON Old man, you all shoot at me like archers: I am your target, and not immune even from your prophetic art. I have long been trafficked by your type, treated as merchandise. Take your profit, trade, if you wish, with the silver-gold of Sardis and the gold of India. But you will not bury that man in a tomb, not even if the eagles of Zeus care to plunder the carrion body and take it to the throne of Zeus; not even in fear of that pollution will I allow him to be buried. I know well that no human has the power to defile the gods. The cleverest of men, aged Teiresias, fall into shameful ruin when they make elegant but shameful speeches for their own advantage.

TEIRESIAS Ah! Does any human have knowledge, or realise...

CREON What? What profound truth are you declaring now?

TEIRESIAS ...the degree to which wisdom is the most precious of possessions?

CREON To the same degree that folly does the most harm.

TEIRESIAS Yet you are riddled with that disease.

CREON I have no wish to return the seer's insult.

TEIRESIAS And yet you do, saying that I make false prophecies.

CREON The whole breed of seers is in love with money.

TEIRESIAS And the race of tyrants is in love with corrupt gain.

CREON Do you realise it is your king that you insult?

TEIRESIAS I know; for it was with my help that you have saved this city.

CREON You are a clever prophet, but you love injustice.

TEIRESIAS You will provoke me to utter the secret of my soul.

Good sense and folly

Haemon and Teiresias extol clear thinking (638–9, 1015). The Chorus think Antigone has been foolish (359, 569), and Creon thinks both sisters lack sense (526–7). Ismene is the only one to acknowledge that reason deserts us when we are in trouble (528–9). Antigone (432), Haemon (705–6) and Teiresias (996, 1018) all accuse Creon of lacking reason; he returns the charge to Haemon (703–4).

Now, despite a show of restraint (1019), Creon seems sure that Teiresias is both corrupt (1005, 1012, 1021, 1028, 1030) and, for all his cleverness (1010), a fool (1017).

1032–3 one born of your loins Haemon's name is not mentioned. Notice that Teiresias uses language reminiscent of Antigone's (see note on 471).

1035–7 Creon did not respect the dead man's honour (*timē*). See note, page 4.

1039 the Furies See note on 569.

Teiresias' judgement

Creon is guilty of two violations of the established order: he has consigned a living person (who belongs in the upper world) to a tomb, and kept a corpse, which belongs in the ground, in the world of the living. Without elaborating the argument, Teiresias seems to equate Creon's offence against Antigone with that against Polyneices. Thus Creon is guilty of a double religious crime; and the Furies of both worlds (1040) will assuredly pursue him for punishment. There will be a death in Creon's own house (1033, 1044).

CREON Speak it! Only do not say it for profit.

TEIRESIAS Do you really think that is my motive?

CREON Be sure you will not buy off my resolve. 1030

TEIRESIAS Know *you* well that you will not live through many more racing journeys of the sun before you give one born of your loins as a corpse in exchange for corpses! For you have cast one from the upper world into the lower, without due honour lodging a life in a tomb, and you keep here a corpse 1035 that belongs to the gods below, forsaken, deprived of rites due, robbed of ceremony. The dead are no concern of yours, nor of the gods above; but you have forced this on them. For this the Destroyers who wait their time lie in wait for you, the Furies of Hades and of the gods, so that you will be seized by these same 1040 disasters.

1044 all the cities This sentence seems irrelevant in our play. In some versions of the story burial was denied to the seven warriors who fought on the walls against the Thebans, and this provoked a second war. In this play, however, only Polyneices has been mentioned, even by Teiresias (986–7). If lines 1044–7 are genuine, it is presumed that some lines have been lost, which would have made their significance clearer.

1053 Teiresias and his guide leave the stage.

1057 I am in turmoil As at line 971, Teiresias' judgemental tone has a powerful effect on Creon.

1057 It is dreadful to yield Creon acknowledges here one of his most significant character traits, which he shares with Antigone (434).

● Do you think that it is significant that on the two occasions when Creon changes his mind (720, see also 723) he is 'alone', with only the Chorus present?

1058–9 the net of Destruction Creon senses the approach of destiny (*atē*, here perhaps – the Greek is obscure – woven by the Fates). He is still responsible for his actions and he will do his best to avoid the catastrophe foretold.

1061 Tell me! I will obey With these simple words Creon submits.

1065 the Harmful Spirits are the Furies.

The Chorus

It is unusual for the Chorus to intervene in the action of a Greek tragedy. Here Creon asks for their advice (1061). They focus his mind on the two tasks that must be done, the need for speed, and that he must do them personally.

● At what point in the scene do you think the Chorus are convinced that Teiresias is right?

○ How do you think they should react to Creon's blasphemy?

And consider well whether I speak under the influence of
silver; for in the passing of no long time there will arise
lamentations of men and women in your house; all the cities
are stirred up with hatred . . . whose torn children have been   1045
hallowed only by dogs and wild animals, or some winged bird,
that carried the unholy stench to the city's hearths.
Such arrows have I fired like an archer at your heart, in anger,
for you have provoked me; arrows that are true, and you shall
not escape their sting.   1050
Boy, lead me home, so that this man can hurl his rage at
younger men, and learn to keep a more peaceful tongue, and a
better mind than the temper he has now.

CHORUS Lord, the man has gone, with a terrible prophecy. But in
all these years while my black hair has turned white, I know   1055
that he has never been a false prophet to the city.

CREON I know it myself, I am in turmoil. It is dreadful to yield,
but terrible too to resist; my heart is beating hard in the net of
Destruction.

CHORUS Son of Menoeceus, you must accept good advice.   1060

CREON So what must I do? Tell me! I will obey.

CHORUS Go and free the girl from her cell of rock, and set up a
tomb for him who lies unburied.

CREON This is your advice? You think that I should yield?

CHORUS Yes, lord, as quickly as possible; the Harmful Spirits are   1065
swift to cut down those in error.

CREON Ah! It is hard, but I give up my resolve; there is no
fighting necessity.

CHORUS Then go and do it; do not entrust it to others.

1070 Take picks As events will show, Creon does not mean that the servants are to go and bury Polyneices, while he frees Antigone: he will do both tasks himself, as ordered (1069). Whether it is fear for Haemon, or a greater sense of guilt as far as Antigone is concerned, it is her release that seems to preoccupy him.

1074 the established laws This seems to be what Antigone was upholding in line 421.
● Has Creon shown any sign of recognising such 'laws' before?

Creon's change of heart
Creon has hitherto respected Teiresias' authority and judgement (967–9) and his concern at the tone of Teiresias' first warning (971) seems to be that of a religious man. But when Teiresias reports the failure of his divination and the disapproval of the gods (988), and in measured language advises Creon to yield, Creon, though he is not incapable of a change of heart (720, 1067), does not take his opportunity. His paranoic suspicion of corruption leads him to unreasonable accusations and, as the two exchange undignified insults, Creon's anger provokes (1027, 1030) Teiresias to a devastating and angry (1048) revelation of the punishment that awaits Creon.
● Why does Creon not give in after Teiresias' first speech?
● Are we to feel that, had Creon yielded then, all would have been well, and Teiresias' prophecy unnecessary?
● What precisely is it that finally causes Creon's change of heart and makes him accept the Chorus' advice?
● Have we seen a development in Creon's character in this scene?
● Do you have hope at the end of the scene that Creon may avert disaster?
● Has the focus of the play shifted to Creon?

The gods
It has been suggested that the gods here show that they are concerned only with the due performance of ritual (Polyneices' burial), not with the fate of humans.
● Is this your impression of this scene? To what extent do you think the gods and Teiresias are interested in Antigone?

CREON I will go as I am. Go, go, servants, all of you! Take picks   1070
and hurry to the place that we can see, over there! Since my
opinion has come round to this, I who bound her will untie
her in person. I am afraid that it is best to live one's life to the
end observing the established laws.

FIFTH CHORAL ODE (5TH *STASIMON*) (1075–1114)

Apparently encouraged by Creon's change of heart, the Chorus invoke Bacchus (Dionysus), the protecting god of Thebes. The ode's form is essentially that of the classical prayer, in which it was customary to list some of the god's titles, cult centres or favourite haunts, as well as some previous services, feats or miracles, in order to establish one's awareness of the god's credentials and the appropriateness of the prayer; and then to explain one's need and to call on the god to appear – and here to cleanse the pollution (1101–5). But the Chorus catch the inherent excitement of Bacchic worship (see below), which they describe, and the mood of their prayer is lively and upbeat.

Bacchus and Thebes

Cadmus, who founded Thebes (see Background to the story, page vii), had a daughter, Semele (1076), with whom Zeus had an affair. Hera, Zeus' jealous wife, tricked Semele into asking Zeus to come to her as he did to Hera. So he came as a thunderbolt (1077): Semele was destroyed (1100), but Zeus saved her unborn baby, called Dionysus or Bacchus, who was later worshipped as a god of nature and fertility, especially associated with wine. Though born (in the Theban legend) in Thebes, his worship came to Greece, according to tradition, from the East, via Lydia and Thrace, introducing an orgiastic cult in which women (called Bacchants 1083, Maenads or Thyiads 1111) sang (1096, 1108) and danced ecstatically on the hills (934, 1112–13).

Bacchus was an ambivalent god. He could bring peace and joy, but he was ruthless towards those who resisted his cult – notably Lycurgus, king of Thrace (922–32), and Pentheus, Cadmus' successor as king of Thebes (see Euripides' *Bacchae*).

1075 God of many names Gods frequently had many titles, reflecting a variety of functions and places with which they were associated. This was particularly true of Dionysus, because his associations were so widespread, but he has only two names in this ode – Bacchus (which came from Lydia) and Iacchus (1114, see note on 1080).

1078 Italy, where there were many Greek colonies, is perhaps mentioned to show the extent of the god's influence.

1080 Deo is another name for Demeter, Earth mother, worshipped at Eleusis on the Saronic gulf near Athens, along with a child Iacchus, who came to be identified with Bacchus. The cult's secret rites, the Eleusinian Mysteries, were thought to confer on its initiates a happy afterlife.

1084 Ismenus was one of the rivers of Thebes.

1085–6 seed/ Of the savage dragon! For the dragon's teeth see Background to the story, page vii.

CHORUS
God of many names,   1075
Glory of the Cadmeian bride,
Child of deep-thundering Zeus!
You who protect famous Italy,
And reign in the welcoming bay
Of Eleusinian Deo!   1080
Bacchus!
You who dwell in Thebes,
The mother city of Bacchants,
By the flowing stream of Ismenus,
On the ground sown with the seed   1085
Of the savage dragon!

Delphi and Bacchus

Delphi, the home of the famous oracle, was also a centre of Bacchus' worship. Above Delphi every other year there was a celebrated night festival in his honour (1113), at which the Bacchants, his female worshippers, carried torches (1088). It was held in the hills above two conspicuous crags (1087), but below the main peak of Mount Parnassus (1104). Corycia (1089) is a large cave high on Parnassus and Castalia (1091) is a stream which flows down the mountain and through Delphi.

1093 Nysa is a name given to several places associated with Bacchus. This one is probably in Euboea, a large island off the east coast of Greece, famous for its vines (1094) and separated from the mainland by a narrow strait, which the god would cross as he travelled between Nysa and Thebes (1105, see map page ix).

1103 Come on your healing way Among his attributes, Bacchus was thought to have healing powers.

Above the twin-peaked crag
You are seen by the smoking flare,
Where the Corycian nymphs go,
The worshippers of Bacchus;   1090
You are seen by the stream of Castalia.
The ivy-covered slopes
Of the mountains of Nysa,
And the shore that is green with grapes
Send you on,   1095
Celebrated by immortal music,
As you come to the city of Thebes.

Thebes, of all cities,
You hold highest in honour,
You and your lightning-struck mother.   1100
Now, as the whole city is gripped
By a violent plague,
Come on your healing way
Over the heights of Parnassus,
Or across the sighing strait.   1105

Hail! Dancing leader
Of the fire-breathing stars,
Guardian of the voices of night!
Child of Zeus,
Appear to us, Lord,   1110
With your attendant Thyiads,
Who dance for you
In their nightlong frenzy,
O Iacchus, giver of gifts!

EXODOS (1115–1326)

This was the name given to the final section of the play, at the end of which the Chorus were led off by an *aulos* player (see note on 937).

The Messenger

In most tragedies a Messenger, usually a slave, reports some important event which has happened indoors or away from the play's setting. Usually his news is exciting or terrible, often the climax of the tragedy, and expressed in highly charged language. The origins of such writing lie in the age of oral epic, when professional bards improvised a repertory of heroic tales, from which grew the *Iliad* and the *Odyssey*. Similar storytelling techniques to those of the bards can be seen in the Messenger speeches: the use of direct speech, colourful metaphor and language and, in particular, vivid detail, which enabled the actor to bring his story to life.

1115 Amphion was an early king of Thebes, who built a wall round the city.

1116 I could praise or find fault with The ominous tone of the Messenger's opening is clear, but we are kept waiting for the details of the disaster. Moralising speeches about the changeability of fortune and the elusiveness of happiness are common in tragedy, especially from the Chorus and the 'simple' characters.

1120 Creon was once to be envied Since we know that Creon has only recently become king (155, 166), his 'absolute control' must include his time as regent (967–8).

Creon – tragic hero?

The Messenger's portrait of Creon, with its fall from prosperity to misfortune and a hint of some crucial mistake or flaw, anticipates Aristotle's outline of the best kind of tragic plot: 'when a man enjoying great reputation and prosperity, but not especially virtuous and just, suffers misfortune, not through vice and wickedness, but because of some error of judgement' (*The Art of Poetry xiii*).
- Does this make you think that the focus of the play is, in fact, Creon?
- How does the choice of Creon as an example of man's vulnerability affect our attitude to him?

1123–5 When a man's happiness forsakes him ... a breathing corpse
- How exactly is this idea relevant to Creon?

1125 breathing corpse This seems to be an ironic echo of Creon's treatment of Antigone (858). Antigone's prayer, that Creon should suffer no more than she (891), is at least in part fulfilled.

MESSENGER Neighbours of the house of Cadmus and Amphion, 1115
there is no human life that I could praise or find fault with as
immune to change. Fate raises and fate lays low the lucky and
unlucky every day. There is no-one who can foresee what is
ordained for mortals.

Creon was once to be envied, in my eyes, having saved this 1120
land of Cadmus from its enemies; and taking absolute control
of the country, he guided it well, blessed with his family of
noble children. Now all is lost. When a man's happiness
forsakes him, I do not rank him among the living, but regard
him as a breathing corpse. Amass great wealth in your house, if 1125
you will, and live amid the trappings of a king; but if joy is
missing, I would not give a man a wisp of smoke for the rest,
compared with happiness.

1130 the living are guilty The Messenger makes a judgement, but again makes us wait for the details. His words seem deliberately elusive (1132); he says that Haemon died 'raging at his father for the murder', but there is no specific mention of Antigone.

Eurydice

Creon's wife has not been mentioned in the play and her entry is something of a surprise.

1141–2 I was coming out As usual, a female character feels the need to explain why she is outside (see note on 15).

1142 Pallas There were two shrines in Thebes to Pallas Athene, goddess of wisdom and female handicrafts.

1146–7 no stranger to misfortune Among all the other troubles of the royal family and the recent war, Eurydice had lost her eldest son (see note on 592, 1268).

1148–9 I will leave out not a word of the truth The Messenger, by his apology, again heightens our expectation of the details to come.

1154 the goddess of the road was Hecate, whose shrines stood mostly where roads met. She was originally a fertility goddess, whose statue stood outside all Athenian homes, and she was important to women, especially at childbirth. It is hard to know the stages by which her cult developed associations with the dead, crossroads, magic and the moon.

1154 Pluto was another name for Hades, god of the underworld, whom the Messenger assumes to be angry at Polyneices' treatment.

1156 we burned what remained The details which we are given conform to the burial rite of the heroic age, in which cremation was the norm. The remaining bones would be washed, wrapped in fat and placed in an urn for burial (under the 'high mound'). The Messenger keeps his description of this part of his story as brief as possible.

CHORUS What is this grief that you bring for the royal house?

MESSENGER They are dead; and the living are guilty of the death.   1130

CHORUS Who is dead? And who killed them? Tell us!

MESSENGER Haemon is dead, his blood spilled by no stranger.

CHORUS Was it his father's hand, or his own?

MESSENGER He died by his own hand, raging at his father for the
murder.   1135

CHORUS O seer, so your prophecy was true!

MESSENGER So it stands; for the rest you must take thought.

CHORUS I see poor Eurydice, Creon's wife. She is coming from
the house, perhaps by chance, perhaps because she has heard
about her son.   1140

EURYDICE Citizens, all of you, I heard your words as I was
coming out to offer prayers to the goddess Pallas. I was just
undoing the bolts to open the door, when the announcement
of some family disaster struck my ears. I fell back in terror into
the arms of my maidservants, and my senses left me. But   1145
whatever the news, tell it again. I will hear it; I am no stranger
to misfortune.

MESSENGER My dear lady, I will speak as a witness, and I will
leave out not a word of the truth. Why should I soothe you
with an account I will later be shown to have invented? The   1150
truth is always the right course.

I escorted your husband as his guide to the far side of the
plain, where the unpitied body of Polyneices still lay, torn by
dogs. We prayed to the goddess of the road and to Pluto to
temper their anger with mercy; we washed the man with holy   1155
rites, and with newly cut branches we burned what remained.
We raised a high mound of his native earth, and then we made
our way towards the hollow chamber of Hades' bride, with its
bed of rock. From far away one of us heard a voice of loud
lamentation beside the chamber where no rites had been paid,   1160
and went to report it to our master, Creon.

1168 the break in the tomb wall The 'tomb' was closed by a pile of stones, which Haemon had broken through. Behind this pile there seems to have been a passage, leading to the mouth of the chamber (1169).

1180–1 I beg you Entreaties were usually accompanied by a ritual gesture: the suppliant might clasp the other's knees or grasp his right hand or touch his chin, and, by so humbling himself, hope to put the other under pressure to grant the request. Haemon's violent rejection of the entreaty (1182) might have seemed shocking to a Greek audience.

1184 furious with himself Not for missing, but ashamed of his lack of control. He warned (699–700) that Antigone's death would cause another; though Creon thought the threat was directed at him, Haemon surely meant himself. He has now come to die with Antigone, having no idea that Creon would disturb him.

1189–90 rites of marriage The phrase recalls Creon's bitter remarks to Haemon ('let this girl marry someone in Hades' 615–16; and 'you will [n]ever marry her while she lives' 698); and Antigone's bleak prophecy that she would marry Acheron (767).

1191 folly is the greatest evil The irony that Creon himself said this (1017), only to be convicted of folly by Teiresias (1018), makes it clear that the Messenger is thinking of Creon, not Haemon. See note on page 78.

As he moved closer, indistinct sounds of wretched crying surrounded him. He cried out in anguish and spoke words of deep grief: 'Ah, in my misery do I see the future? Am I going on the most unhappy journey now of any road that I have travelled? The voice of my son gives me hope! But go nearer, servants, quickly, stand around the tomb and look! Go in through the break in the tomb wall where the rock has been torn away, to the very mouth of the chamber! See if it is Haemon's voice I recognise, or if I am deluded by the gods!' We went to look, at our despairing master's command. In the furthest part of the tomb, we saw her hanging by the neck, suspended by the linen noose of a garment; and we saw him, embracing her, with his arms around her waist, crying out at the loss of his bride beneath the earth, at his father's deeds, and at his doomed marriage.

Creon, when he saw the two of them, gave a bitter cry. He went in to them, and called in a voice of grief: 'Ah, my poor son, what have you done! What were you thinking of? What catastrophe destroyed your mind? Come out, my son, I beg you on my knees!'

But the boy glared at him with savage eyes, spat in his face, and making no reply he drew his cross-hilted sword; his father ran, and he missed. Then, furious with himself, the ill-fated boy without hesitation used his weight to drive half the length of his sword through his side; and while he lived he clasped the girl in his weakening embrace. Gasping, he poured out a swift stream of blood that fell on her white cheek.

Corpse lies embracing corpse. The poor man has won his rites of marriage in the house of Hades, showing to the world that folly is the greatest evil that can fall upon a man.

1165

1170

1175

1180

1185

1190

1192 The woman has gone Eurydice, after a very brief appearance, leaves in silence. The effectiveness of her silent exit is heightened by the dialogue which follows.

- Why do you think Sophocles introduced the character of Eurydice, rather than let us simply hear of her fate from the Messenger (1240)?

1197 handmaids She will set up the ritual keening in the household (see note on Honours due to the dead, page 4).

1198 do anything unseemly like (presumably) grieving in public.

Creon's return
As the Messenger enters the house (1203), Creon arrives with Haemon's corpse. The text suggests that Creon holds the body (1205, 1237, 1261), but this need mean no more than that he touches it or holds its hand. It seems probable that he is accompanied by attendants who carry the body.

Second *kommos*
A *kommos* (see 758) follows, in which – unusually – Creon's highly emotional *sung* grief is interspersed with lines *spoken* by the Chorus and the Messenger. This serves to highlight Creon's isolation; it suggests that no-one else enters into his grief, and focuses our attention on his coming to terms with his guilt.

1209 the mistake was his own The Chorus, like the Messenger (1130, 1191), see Creon as the architect of his own downfall.

Responsibility
Just as the Chorus could see Antigone's suffering as a part of the family curse (818) and at the same time say that her 'self-willed temper' destroyed her (841), so Creon can talk of 'a god [...] who struck my head' (1229), yet acknowledge his own stubbornness (1211) and folly (1217, 1224). This reference to an unnamed god does not excuse his responsibility for Haemon's death (1222–4).

F. Murray Abraham as Creon with the dead Haemon, New York Shakespeare Festival production.

CHORUS What do you make of this? The woman has gone back in, before saying anything good or bad.

MESSENGER I am surprised myself. I can only hope that, after hearing the grief of her son, she will think it not right to grieve 1195
in front of the city; but beneath her own roof she will reveal the sorrow of the house to her handmaids, for them to grieve. She is not so lacking in judgement as to do anything unseemly.

CHORUS I do not know. But to me too much silence seems no less ominous than empty cries of grief. 1200

MESSENGER Then I will go into the house and find out if she is hiding some secret in her passionate heart. For you are right; perhaps an excess of silence can bode ill.

CHORUS   Now comes our master himself,
               Carrying a memorial 1205
           That needs no explanation;
              Not, if it may be said,
             Another man's madness,
          For the mistake was his own.

CREON   Oh! 1210
            Stubborn and fatal errors
           Of a mind without reason!
               Look on us,
              In one family
          The killer and the slain. 1215
           Alas for the misery
             Of my decisions!
                  Oh!
            My son, so young,
          Your life cut short! 1220
               Ah! Ah!
          You are dead and gone,
            Not through your folly,
              But through mine.

CHORUS   Alas, too late you seem to see justice! 1225

Learning from suffering

It was a commonplace of Greek moral thought that we can learn from suffering. Haemon, the Chorus and Teiresias all impressed on Creon the importance of listening to advice (659–60, 670–1, 1000); Antigone (once, 889–90) acknowledged that she might be wrong and, if so, she would learn from her suffering. For Creon to say 'I have learned my lesson' (1227) represents a complete change of heart.

- Do Creon's submissiveness and acceptance of his guilt make him a more sympathetic figure?
- Why is Creon concerned only about Haemon? (See note on Fathers and sons, page 48.)

The Second Messenger

Whether or not we think of him as the same Messenger as the first, a servant now arrives with yet more bad news, of Eurydice's suicide. As before, the details are delayed.

1240 true mother This may mean that Eurydice identified herself with her son.

1242 Hades/ That cannot be appeased Haemon's death has not atoned for the treatment of Polyneices' corpse. Hades demands yet more dead in his haven/harbour.

1249 boy Creon seems to be addressing the Messenger, not Haemon's corpse. It was not uncommon to call slaves 'boy'.

1254 You can see it There was a device in the Greek theatre, the *ekkuklēma*, a platform which could be wheeled out from the central upstage door of the stage to reveal an interior tableau or scene. Here it would have shown the dead Eurydice with her sword, beside an altar.

CREON   Alas!
                   I have learned my lesson,
                        Wretched fool!
            It was a god, then, who struck my head
                     A crushing blow,   1230
            And shook me onto a savage course,
                           Alas,
            Overturning and stamping on my joy.
            Ah! The suffering, the harsh suffering
                        Of mankind!   1235

MESSENGER Master, you have more in store than you have here:
    it seems you have come with horror in your hands, and you
    are soon to see more in the house.
CREON What is there yet more terrible than these terrors?
MESSENGER Your wife is dead, the true mother of this corpse,   1240
    poor woman, with wounds still fresh.

CREON   Oh harbour of Hades
                   That cannot be appeased,
                Why, why are you destroying me?
                You, bringer of agonising news,   1245
                   What are you saying?
                Ah, you have killed a man
                     Already dead!
                What are you saying, boy?
            What new death are you telling me?   1250
                       Ah! Ah!
                   My wife's death
               Heaped upon destruction?

CHORUS   You can see it;
                It is no longer hidden within.   1255

CREON   Alas!
                   This is the second evil
               That I look upon in my misery.
                   What, then, what fate
                Still lies ahead of me?   1260

1266 the altar would be that of Zeus Herkaios in the courtyard of the house (447); the sword may have been one used for sacrifice.

1268 Megareus must be the older son (see note on 1146). In Aeschylus' *Seven against Thebes* he is one of the defenders of Thebes. As a wife and mother, Eurydice bewails the fact that she has lost both her sons and will have no grandchildren.

1269 you who killed her sons All shedding of blood incurred pollution. To kill a relative was a worse sin, and Medea, in Euripides' *Medea*, called her murder of her sons 'the most unholy crime'. To be accused in this way (also 1278) is the climax of horror for Creon.

1279 the other's The natural interpretation of the Greek is that this refers to Megareus' death (see note on 1146, 1268), but it is not clear why Creon could be blamed for it. The alternative, rejected by most scholars, is to interpret the phrase as a reference to Antigone.
● Why do you think editors reject the idea that it refers to Antigone?

Creon's repentance
Creon not only proclaims his guilt (1283–9); he prays for death (1295–1301). He is 'less than nothing', a broken man, reminding us perhaps of Haemon's taunt (655–8) that, when arrogant men are laid open, 'they are seen to be empty'. He acknowledges his folly and his responsibility for Haemon's and Eurydice's deaths (1308–19).

Even as I hold my son in my arms,
In misery,
I see her corpse before me!
Ah, poor mother!
Ah, my son!   1265

MESSENGER Stabbed with a sharp blade beside the altar she closed
her eyes in darkness. She bewailed the fruitless marriage of
Megareus who died before, and then of this boy here; and last of
all she sang a litany of your evil actions, you who killed her sons.

CREON   Ah!   1270
I shudder in terror!
Why does someone
Not strike through my heart
With a two-edged sword?
I am desolate,   1275
Ah!
Enfolded in desolate pain!

MESSENGER Yes, you were charged guilty of this boy's death, and
of the other's, by the dead woman here.
CREON How did she die?   1280
MESSENGER She stabbed herself in the heart with her own hand,
once she heard the shrill mourning for her son's fate.

CREON   Alas, the guilt can never be attached
To another mortal
To relieve me.   1285
For it was I,
Oh! Oh!
I who killed you.
I admit the truth.
Servants, take me away quickly,   1290
Take me away from here,
I who am less than nothing.

CHORUS Your command is good, if there can be good amid
disaster; quickest is best when evils are before us.

Creon's character

The Chorus highlight Creon's arrogance (1324). A ruler who can say that the state belongs to him (684) is certainly arrogant. But he has other qualities which are perhaps as significant in his downfall. He is a sadistic and cruel man (280, 711) with an obsessive concern for order and discipline (especially 606–7, 629–33). He is frightened by any threat to his authority, especially from a woman. Inflexible, sure that he is in the right, and afraid of seeming weak, he does not listen to others, especially the young and his subjects. All of this suggests a basic insecurity, which leads to his many errors of judgement.

He is not irreligious, but he makes light of some claims of religion (which Antigone upholds), makes remarks which seem blasphemous, and even accuses Teiresias of venality.

● Is Creon brought down by Antigone, the gods or himself?

Ironies

There are ironies in Creon's fate. The man who put the state before his family destroys his family and the order which he values, and leaves the state 'sick' (985). He claims that stubborn wills can be broken: he is thinking of Antigone, but it is he who is broken, and worsted – as he most feared – by a woman. He tells Haemon to 'Spit her out' (615), but it is on Creon that Haemon spits. 'Evil comes to seem good to one/ Whose mind a god leads to ruin' (588–9) say the Chorus, thinking of Antigone, but with hindsight the words have more relevance to Creon.

CREON   Let it come, let it come!   1295
                   Let the fairest fate that I could meet
                          Now come to pass,
                    The fate that brings my last day;
                          The best fate possible.
                     Let it come, let it come!   1300
                     That I may see no other day!

CHORUS That lies in the future. We must deal with the
   immediate needs; the future concerns those whose concern
   it is.
CREON All that I want, I have uttered in that prayer.   1305
CHORUS Then make no more prayers. There is no escape for
   mortals from disaster that is destined.

CREON   Lead me away,
                            A foolish man,
                         Who against my will   1310
                         Killed you, my son,
                       And also you, my wife.
                            Ah, grief!
                   I do not know on which to look,
                          On what to lean.   1315
                     Everything in my hands
                     Has twisted from my grip,
                     And on my head has fallen
                     A fate that is hard to bear.

The Chorus' verdict

The Chorus prepare to assume their responsibilities, the burial of the corpses (1302–3). They resort to conventional piety: the future is the concern of the gods (1303–4), to whom no irreverence must be shown (1322–3). In view of Creon's acknowledgement of his folly (1217, 1224, 1309), it is no surprise that they stress the importance of wisdom (1320). Their final judgement, that Creon's pride and arrogance have been punished and he forced to learn wisdom (1324–6), recalls their own words in the *parodos*, that 'Zeus hates the boasts of a proud tongue' (119), and fits Creon's fate into the established morality.

Summing up

The play presents a clash between two people, both committed to a fixed position and unwilling to give way. Their conflict results in three deaths; Creon survives, a 'breathing corpse' (1125).

- Is the main theme of the play an irreconcilable clash of wills or is it the downfall of Creon?
- If it is the former, does it matter that Antigone makes her final exit from the stage so early?
- Why do you think Sophocles does not bring the corpse of Antigone back to the stage at the end of the play?

CHORUS   Wisdom is by far   1320
The greatest part of happiness.
No irreverence
Must be shown to the gods.
The mighty words of overproud men
With mighty blows are punished,   1325
And, with old age, teach wisdom.

Synopsis of the play

PROLOGUE (1–90)

Antigone takes Ismene away from the palace to tell her that Creon, after the defeat of the Argives, has given their brother Eteocles an honourable burial, but that their other brother, Polyneices, who fought with the Argives, is to be left unburied. Creon has condemned to death by stoning anyone who mourns or tries to bury Polyneices. Antigone asks Ismene to help her to bury him. She is contemptuous of Ismene's cautious refusal and looks forward if necessary to a noble, martyr's death.

PARODOS (91–158)

The Chorus of elders enter. They have been summoned to hear a proclamation by Creon. They salute the dawn, and exult in the Theban victory. Zeus has punished the *hubris* of the Argives, and the victory is total, except for the shared death of the two brothers.

FIRST EPISODE (159–305)

Creon commends the elders for their loyalty through many crises, the last of which – the death of Oedipus' two sons – leaves him king. He lays out the qualities which he admires in a ruler and the principles on which he intends to govern. He has no respect for the man who puts a loved one before the state. The safety of the state is paramount. Eteocles will have a hero's burial; the corpse of Polyneices, his traitorous brother, will be left to rot. Anyone who disobeys the edict will die.

A sentry arrives with news that the corpse has been buried by a covering of dust. Whoever did it left no signs. Creon angrily dismisses the Chorus' suggestion that it may be the work of the gods. He is sure that the guards have been bribed by those in the city who resent his rule. He threatens the sentry that he will hang him alive, if he does not find the culprit.

FIRST CHORAL ODE (306–359)

The Chorus express the marvel of man's resourcefulness. He has subdued the natural world and learnt to kill and tame animals; then developed his intellectual and social skills to create civilisation; there is only death from which he has found no escape. His skills can be put to good use or bad: if he observes the laws of the state and the justice which men swear by the gods to keep, he makes his state great; the man who recklessly embraces evil has no state.

SECOND EPISODE (360–546)

The Sentry returns with Antigone. He reports that the guards swept the covering of dirt from Polyneices' corpse and resumed their vigil. After a strange whirlwind, Antigone was seen performing burial rites. She did not resist arrest. Now she defiantly says that she has obeyed the unwritten laws of the gods, which have more authority than Creon's decree. Creon is incensed by her arrogance. He condemns both Antigone and Ismene to 'the most terrible death'. Antigone thinks it glorious to bury her brother. Creon cannot believe that a traitor deserves the same treatment as a patriot.

Ismene is brought in, wanting to share Antigone's responsibility and fate. Antigone repudiates her, saying that, by her initial refusal to help, Ismene chose to live. Ismene asks Creon if he will really kill his son's betrothed: yes, he says, he could not have his son married to a criminal.

SECOND CHORAL ODE (547–596)

The Chorus in sombre mood sing of the curse (*atē*) which can remorselessly destroy a family, generation after generation. Now the sisters, the last survivors of Labdacus' clan, are destroyed by foolish ideas. Zeus is invincible. No human crime or aggrandisement can escape punishment: god, through men's ambition and desire, controls their minds and leads them to destruction.

THIRD EPISODE (597–728)

Haemon arrives, professing dutiful submission. Creon warns him against the allure of an evil woman. Antigone is a relative, but she must die. All must be treated alike. The same discipline and obedience, which are important in the family, are necessary in public life. Obedience tends to success, disobedience to ruin. So obey the rules and don't give in to a woman. If you are going to lose power, lose it to a man.

Haemon tells his father that the citizens secretly approve of Antigone's actions, and advises him not to be inflexible. Creon is indignant that anyone else should tell him how to govern the state, despising Haemon for taking a woman's part. Haemon leaves, promising that Antigone's death will cause another.

Then, in answer to the Chorus' question whether he will kill both the sisters, Creon spares Ismene and decides to immure Antigone in a chamber of rock.

THIRD CHORAL ODE (729–757)

The Chorus address Eros, the god of sexual desire, whom neither gods nor mortals can resist. Love has caused this quarrel between Creon and Haemon. It is a destructive force, capriciously and violently driving its victims to madness, injustice and disgrace.

FOURTH EPISODE (758–908)

In a lyrical dialogue with the Chorus, Antigone laments that she will die unmarried. She traces the family curse, recalling her parents' incestuous marriage and the doomed marriage of her brother Polyneices. The Chorus remind her that it is her own self-will which has destroyed her, but she continues to lament that she dies unmarried and unwept. Creon orders her to be led away to her 'tomb'. He declares himself guiltless.

Antigone imagines herself, as the last of her family, lovingly reunited with them in death. Finally she calls the Chorus of elders to witness what she suffers for her piety.

FOURTH CHORAL ODE (909–961)

The Chorus look for mythical parallels to Antigone's situation – the princess Danae; Lycurgus, king of the Edonians; and the innocent Cleopatra – none of whom could avoid their destined fate.

FIFTH EPISODE (962–1074)

Teiresias, the seer, enters. He tells Creon that all his attempts at augury and burnt offerings have failed, indicating that, through Creon's fault, the city is sick, polluted by carrion from Polyneices' corpse. Creon must yield, not persist in his error.

Creon refuses to bury the corpse. Enraged by Creon's repeated accusations of corruption, Teiresias warns him that 'one born of Creon's loins' will soon die. Creon has consigned a living person to a tomb, and kept a corpse, which belongs in the ground, in the world of the living. He is guilty of a double religious crime. As Teiresias leaves, Creon in alarm asks the Chorus for advice. They tell him to free Antigone and bury Polyneices. Creon succumbs.

FIFTH CHORAL ODE (1075–1114)

The Chorus invoke Bacchus (Dionysus), the protecting god of Thebes, to come and cleanse the pollution.

EXODOS (1115–1326)

A Messenger arrives to tell of the death of Haemon. Eurydice enters to hear the details. Creon and his servants, having buried Polyneices' remains, went to Antigone's 'tomb', where they found her hanging, Haemon clinging to her body. Seeing his father, he spat at him, then fell on his own sword. He died, embracing Antigone. Eurydice, without saying anything, goes indoors.

Creon enters with Haemon's body. He mourns his folly and his son's death. As Creon acknowledges that he has learnt his lesson, another Messenger announces the death of Eurydice: accusing Creon of her two sons' deaths, she has stabbed herself. Her corpse is brought on.

Creon accepts responsibility for her death and asks to be taken away to his own death. The Chorus prefer that events should take their course. Their final judgement is that the mighty words of overproud men are punished with mighty blows.

Pronunciation of names

To attempt an authentic pronunciation of classical Greek names presents great difficulties. It is perhaps easiest to accept the conventional anglicised versions of the familiar names (e.g. Ares, Zeus). The key below offers help with all the names in the play, which will give a reasonable overall consistency. Note that the stress occurs on the italicised syllable.

KEY

ay – as in 'hay'   *ō* – long 'o', as in 'go'
ē – as in 'hair'   *ch* – as in Scottish 'loch'
ī – as in 'die'

Acheron	*A*-cher-ōn	Hades	*Hay*-dees
Amphion	Am-*phi*-ōn	Haemon	*Hī*-mōn
Antigone	An-*ti*-go-nē	Iacchus	I-*a*-kus
Ares	*Air*-reez	Ismene	Is-*mē*-nē
Argives	*Ar*-gīvs	Labdacus	*Lab*-da-kus
Bacchus	*Bak*-kus	Lycurgus	Lī-*kur*-gus
Boreas	Bo-re-*as*	Megareus	*Me*-ga-ryus
Bosporus	*Bos*-po-rus	Menoeceus	Me-*noi*-kyus
Cadmeian	Kad-*may*-an	Nysa	*Nī*-sa
Cadmus	*Kad*-mus	Oedipus	*Ee*-di-pus
Castalia	Kas-*tal*-i-a	Pallas	*Pal*-las
Corycia	Kō-*ri*-si-a	Parnassus	Par-*nass*-us
Creon	*Kre*-ōn	Persephone	Per-*se*-fo-nē
Danae	Da-*na*-ē	Phrygia	*Fri*-ji-a
Deo	*Dē*-ō	Polyneices	Po-li-*nī*-sees
Dionysus	Dī-o-*ni*-sus	Salmydessus	Sal-mi-*dēs*-sus
Dirce	*Der*-sē	Sipylus	Si-*pi*-lus
Dryas	*Dri*-as	Tantalus	*Tan*-ta-lus
Edonians	Ē-*dō*-ni-ans	Teiresias	Tī-*re*-si-as
Eleusinian	E-lyu-*si*-ni-an	Thebes	Theebs
Erechtheidae	E-*rech*-thay-i-dī	Thrace	Thrays
Erechtheus	E-*rech*-thyus	Thyiads	Thi-*i*-ads
Eteocles	*E*-te-o-klees	Zeus	Zyoos
Eurydice	Yu-*ri*-di-sē		

Introduction to the Greek Theatre

Theātron, the Greek word that gave us 'theatre' in English, meant both 'viewing place' and the assembled viewers. These ancient viewers (*theātai*) were in some ways very different from their modern counterparts. For a start, they were participants in a religious festival, and they went to watch plays only on certain days in the year, when shows were put on in honour of Dionysus. At Athens, where drama developed many of its most significant traditions, the main Dionysus festival, held in the spring, was one of the most important events in the city's calendar, attracting large numbers of citizens and visitors from elsewhere in the Greek world. It is not known for certain whether women attended; if any did, they were more likely to be visitors than the wives of Athenian citizens.

The festival was also a great sporting occasion. Performances designed to win the god's favour needed spectators to witness and share in the event, just as the athletic contests did at Olympia or Delphi, and one of the ways in which the spectators got involved was through competition. What they saw were three sets of three tragedies plus a satyr play, five separate comedies and as many as twenty song-and-dance performances called dithyrambs, put on in honour of Dionysus by choruses representing the different 'tribes' into which the citizen body was divided. There was a contest for each different event, with the dithyramb choruses divided into men's and boys' competitions, and a panel of judges determined the winners. The judges were appointed to act on behalf of the city; no doubt they took some notice of the way the audience responded on each occasion. Attendance at these events was on a large scale: we should be thinking of football crowds rather than typical theatre audiences in the modern world.

Like football matches, dramatic festivals were open-air occasions, and the performances were put on in daylight rather than with stage lighting in a darkened auditorium. The ideal performance space in these circumstances was a hollow hillside to seat spectators, with a flat area at the bottom (*orchēstra*) in which the chorusmen could spread out for their dancing and singing and which could be closed off by a stage-building (*skēnē*) acting simultaneously as backdrop, changing room and sounding board. Effective acoustics and good sight-lines were achieved by the kind of design represented in Fig. A on page 111, the theatre of Dionysus at Athens. The famous stone theatre at Epidaurus (Fig. B), built about 330 BC, and often taken as typical, has a circular *orchēstra*, but in the fifth century it was normal practice for

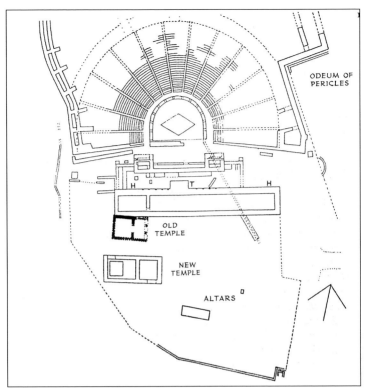

Fig. A. The theatre of Dionysus at Athens.

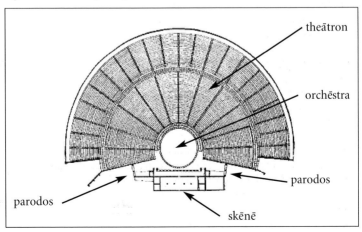

Fig. B. The theatre at Epidaurus (fourth century BC).

theatres to have a low wooden stage in front of the *skēnē*, for use by the actors, who also interacted with the chorus in the *orchēstra*.

Song and dance by choruses and the accompanying music of the piper were integral to all these types of performance and not just to the dithyramb. In tragedy there were 12 (later 15) chorusmen, in comedy 24, and in dithyramb 50; plays were often named after their chorus: Aeschylus' *Persians*, Euripides' *Bacchae*, Aristophanes' *Birds* are familiar examples. The rhythmic movements, groupings and singing of the chorus contributed crucially to the overall impact of each show, ensuring that there was always an animated stage picture even when only one or two actors were in view. The practice of keeping the number of speaking actors normally restricted to three, with doubling of roles by the same actor where necessary, looks odd at first sight, but it makes sense in the special circumstance of Greek theatrical performance. Two factors are particularly relevant: first the use of masks, which was probably felt to be fundamental to shows associated with the cult of Dionysus and which made it easy for an actor to take more than one part within a single play, and second the need to concentrate the audience's attention by keeping the number of possible speakers limited. In a large, open acting area some kind of focusing device is important if the spectators are always to be sure where to direct their gaze. The Greek plays that have survived, particularly the tragedies, are extremely economical in their design, with no sub-plots or complications in the action which audiences might find distracting or confusing. Acting style, too, seems to have relied on large gestures and avoidance of fussy detail; we know from the size of some of the surviving theatres that many spectators would be sitting too far away to catch small-scale gestures or stage business. Some plays make powerful use of props, like Ajax's sword, Philoctetes' bow, or the head of Pentheus in *Bacchae*, but all these are carefully chosen to be easily seen and interpreted.

Above all, actors seem to have depended on their highly trained voices in order to captivate audiences and stir their emotions. By the middle of the fifth century there was a prize for the best actor in the tragic competition, as well as for the playwright and the financial sponsor of the performance (*chorēgos*), and comedy followed suit a little later. What was most admired in the leading actors who were entitled to compete for this prize was the ability to play a series of different and very demanding parts in a single day and to be a brilliant singer as well as a compelling speaker of verse: many of the main parts involve solo songs or complex exchanges between actor and chorus. Overall, the best plays and performances must have offered audiences a great charge of energy and excitement: the chance to see a group of chorusmen dancing and singing in a sequence of different guises, as young maidens, old counsellors, ecstatic maenads, and exuberant satyrs; to watch scenes in which supernatural beings – gods, Furies, ghosts – come into contact with human beings; to listen to intense debates and hear the blood-curdling offstage cries that heralded the arrival of a messenger with an account of terrifying deeds within, and then to see the bodies brought out and witness the lamentations. Far more 'happened' in most plays than we can easily imagine from the bare text on the page; this must help to account for the continuing appeal of drama throughout antiquity and across the Greco-Roman world.

From the fourth century onwards dramatic festivals became popular wherever there were communities of Greek speakers, and other gods besides Dionysus were honoured with performances of plays. Actors, dancers and musicians organised themselves for professional touring – some of them achieved star status and earned huge fees – and famous old plays were revived as part of the repertoire. Some of the plays that had been first performed for Athenian citizens in the fifth century became classics for very different audiences – women as well as men, Latin speakers as well as Greeks – and took on new kinds of meaning in their new environment. But theatre was very far from being an antiquarian institution: new plays, new dramatic forms like mime and pantomime, changes in theatre design, staging, masks and costumes all demonstrate its continuing vitality in the Hellenistic and Roman periods. Nearly all the Greek plays that have survived into modern times are ones that had a long theatrical life in antiquity; this perhaps helps to explain why modern actors, directors and audiences have been able to rediscover their power.

For further reading: entries in *Oxford Classical Dictionary* (3rd edition) under 'theatre staging, Greek' and 'tragedy, Greek'; J.R. Green, 'The theatre', Ch. 7 of *The Cambridge Ancient History, Plates to Volumes V and VI*, Cambridge, 1994; Richard Green and Eric Handley, *Images of the Greek Theatre*, London, 1995; Rush Rehm, *Greek Tragic Theatre*, London and New York, 1992; P.E. Easterling (ed.), *The Cambridge Companion to Greek Tragedy*, Cambridge, 1997; David Wiles, *Tragedy in Athens*, Cambridge, 1997.

Pat Easterling

Time line

Dates of selected authors and extant works

12th Century BC	**The Trojan war**	
8th Century BC	**HOMER**	• *The Iliad* • *The Odyssey*
5th Century BC 490–479 431–404	**The Persian wars** **The Peloponnesian wars**	

c. 525/4–456/5
 	
472
 	
456
	AESCHYLUS	(In probable order.)
		
		• *Persians*
		• *Seven against Thebes*
		• *Suppliants*
		• **Oresteia Trilogy:**
		  Agamemnon, Choephoroi
		  Eumenides
		• *Prometheus Bound*

c. 496/5–406 409 401 (posthumous)	**SOPHOCLES**	(Undated plays are in alphabetical order.) • *Ajax* • *Oedipus Tyrannus* • *Antigone* • *Trachiniae* • *Electra* • *Philoctetes* • *Oedipus at Colonus*
c. 490/80–407/6 438 (1st production 455) 431 428 415 412 409 ?408 ?408–6	**EURIPIDES**	(In probable order.) • *Alcestis* • *Medea* • *Heracleidae* • *Hippolytus* • *Andromache* • *Hecuba* • *Suppliant Women* • *Electra* • *Trojan Women* • *Heracles* • *Iphigenia among the Taurians* • *Helen* • *Ion* • *Phoenissae* • *Orestes* • *Cyclops* (satyr-play) • *Bacchae* • *Iphigenia at Aulis*
460/50–*c.* 386 411 405	**ARISTOPHANES**	(Selected works.) • *Thesmophoriazusae* • *Lysistrata* • *Frogs*
4th Century BC 384–322	**ARISTOTLE**	(Selected works.) • *The Art of Poetry*

Index

Bold numbers refer to pages. Other numbers are line references.